CRAZY HORSE

Warrior Spirit of the Sioux

TONY HOLLIHAN

FOLK
LORE
PUBLISHING

The Publisher: Folklore Publishing
Distributed by Lone Pine Publishing
10145–81 Ave., Edmonton, AB   T6E 1W9   Canada
Toll Free: 800-661-9017   **Website:** www.folklorepublishing.com

National Library of Canada Cataloguing in Publication Data
Hollihan, K. Tony (Kelvin Tony), 1964–
  Crazy Horse / K. Tony Hollihan.
  (Legends series)
  Includes bibliographical references.
  ISBN 1-894864-08-5

  1. Crazy Horse, ca. 1842–1877. 2. Oglala Indians—Kings and rulers—Biography. I. Title. II. Series: Legends series (Edmonton, Alta.)
E99.O3C723 2003   978.004'9752'0092   C2003-910598-9

Project Director: Faye Boer

Photography credits: Every effort has been made to accurately credit the sources of photographs. Any errors or omissions should be directed to the publisher for changes in future editions. *Photographs courtesy of* AZUSA Publishing, Englewood, CO (p. 222); Bancroft Library (p. 47, 32403); Denver Public Library (p. 213, X-33351); Eyewire (p. 67); Glenbow Archives, Calgary, Canada (p. 77, NA-1133-8); Library of Congress (p. 19, USZ62-17590; p. 30, USZ62-100354; p. 36, USZ62-094187; p. 44, USZ62-105381; p. 99, USZ62-86442; p. 114, USZ62-101621; p. 116, USZ62-193; p. 128, B813-2124; p. 135, USZ62-91032; p. 182, BH82601-30695; p. 185, USZ62-54652; p. 203, USZ62-109592; p. 205, USZ62- 088633; p. 208, USZ62-131515; p. 211, USZ62-122957); Minnesota Historical Society (p. 121, AV1988.45.153); Montana Historical Society (p. 196, 943-884); National Anthropological Archives, Smithsonian Institution (p. 157, 44110); National Archives, Old Military and Civil Records (p. 143; p. 144); National Archives and Records, Still Pictures Branch (p. 72, NWDNS-111-B-4693; p. 162, NWDNS-111-B-1769; p. 164, NWDNS-11-B-4169; p. 166, NWDNS-111-B-67; p. 180; NWDNS-111-B-2209); National Museum of the American Indian, Smithsonian Institution (p. 15, 16/1351); Nebraska State Historical Society (p. 64, RG1227.ph-25.2); p. 93, RG2063-5.1; p. 125, RG2955.ph-25; p. 148, RG2095.ph-0.80); *A Pictographic History of the Oglala Sioux* by Amos Bad Heart Bull, text by Helen H. Blish, reproduced with permission of the University of Nebraska Press © renewed 1995 (p. 108, p. 190, p. 225); *The American West in the Nineteenth Century*, 1992, Dover Publications (p. 139; p. 193) University of Nebraska-Lincoln Libraries, Archives & Special Collections (p. 227).

COMMITTED TO THE DEVELOPMENT OF CULTURE AND THE ARTS

PC: P6

For Finley,

May You Too

Live Great Dreams

ACKNOWLEDGMENTS

WHAT DOES A BOOK such as this require? It needs vision, opportunity and advice. It also demands a dedicated and talented team, a great description of those working on the Legends series. Thanks to all the staff of Folklore Publishing, especially Faye Boer.

There are many whose words and actions have contributed to my doing what I've always wanted: David Kales, who was great for insights into so many historical subjects; Tim Wild, who stood fast with me before a pair of sixes; Mrs. Abbott, Mr. Coultas and Mr. Parsons, teachers from long ago who fired my interest in history and writing; Joe Cherwinski, David Hall and David Wangler, more recent teachers who helped me hone my craft; my encouraging parents, Roslyn and Kelvin; my uncle, whose influence is greater than might be supposed; and my wife Laureen, who is always there with support and time.

I'd also like to acknowledge the proud, responsible and honest people in this story. Their strength of character might be used as a measuring stick for many of us.

To those I've overlooked, my omission does not undermine my appreciation.

Title page photo: Thanks to Craig Dockrill for this photo of the Crazy Horse Memorial, located in the Black Hills of South Dakota. It is the world's largest sculpture and was begun in 1948 by sculptor Korczak Ziolkowski. His work on the 563-foot-high mountain carving has been continued by his family since his death in 1982.

TABLE OF CONTENTS

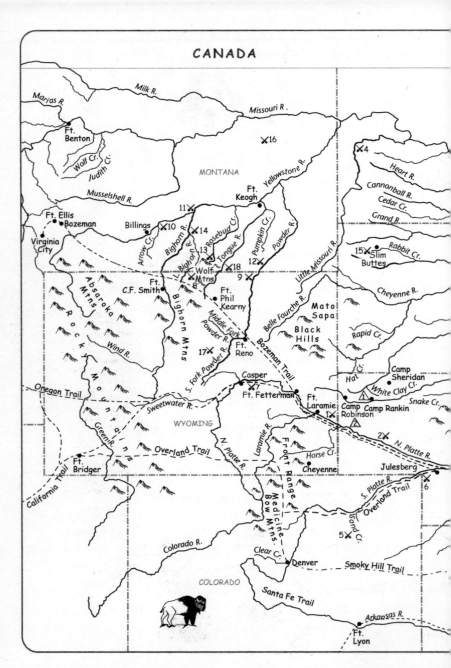

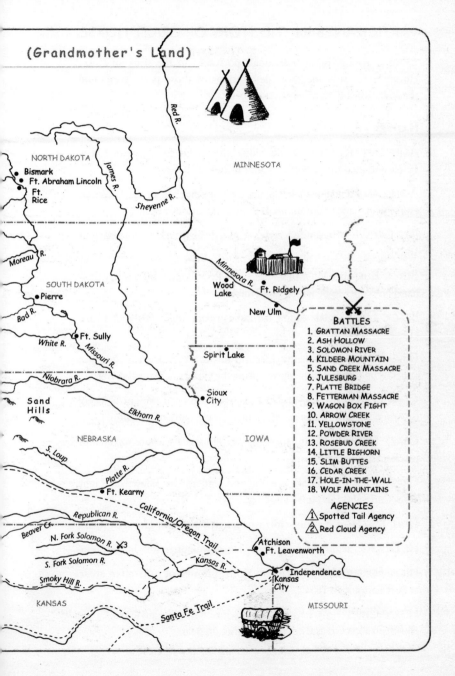

(Grandmother's Land)

NORTH DAKOTA
Bismark
Ft. Abraham Lincoln
Ft. Rice

MINNESOTA

Red R.

James R.

Sheyenne R.

Moreau R.

SOUTH DAKOTA
Pierre

Bad R.

Minnesota R.
Wood Lake
Ft. Ridgely
New Ulm

White R.
Ft. Sully

Missouri R.

Niobrara R.

Sand Hills

Spirit Lake

Sioux City

Elkhorn R.

IOWA

NEBRASKA

S. Loup

Platte R.

Ft. Kearny

Republican R.

Beaver Cr.

N. Fork Solomon R.   ✕3

S. Fork Solomon R.

Smoky Hill R.

California/Oregon Trail

Kansas R.

Atchison
Ft. Leavenworth

Independence
Kansas City

KANSAS

Santa Fe Trail

MISSOURI

BATTLES
1. GRATTAN MASSACRE
2. ASH HOLLOW
3. SOLOMON RIVER
4. KILDEER MOUNTAIN
5. SAND CREEK MASSACRE
6. JULESBURG
7. PLATTE BRIDGE
8. FETTERMAN MASSACRE
9. WAGON BOX FIGHT
10. ARROW CREEK
11. YELLOWSTONE
12. POWDER RIVER
13. ROSEBUD CREEK
14. LITTLE BIGHORN
15. SLIM BUTTES
16. CEDAR CREEK
17. HOLE-IN-THE-WALL
18. WOLF MOUNTAINS

AGENCIES
⚠1 Spotted Tail Agency
⚠2 Red Cloud Agency

PARTICIPANTS IN THE STORY OF CRAZY HORSE

There is a long list of individuals portrayed in the story of Crazy Horse. Here are some short descriptions of those participants and their relationship to others in the story.

NATIVES

AMERICAN HORSE——Oglala Sioux chief who fought with Crazy Horse and died in the Battle of Slim Buttes in 1876

AMERICAN HORSE——Oglala Sioux chief and nephew of the American Horse who died at Slim Buttes. He was an advocate of peace.

BIG CROW——Cheyenne warrior who led the attack on Julesburg in 1865

BLACK BUFFALO WOMAN——niece of Red Cloud who left her husband No Water to be with Crazy Horse.

BLACK ELK——Oglala Sioux *wichasha wakan* and relative of Crazy Horse

BLACK KETTLE——Cheyenne chief and advocate of peace. His band was attacked by Colonel Chivington during the Cheyenne-Arapaho War.

CONQUERING BEAR——Brulé Sioux appointed head chief of all Sioux by American authorities at 1851 Horse Creek treaty negotiations

CRAZY HORSE——Crazy Horse's father. He was a *wichasa wakan* and was later known as Worm.

CRAZY HORSE——Oglala warrior and leader; also known as Light Hair, Curly and His Horse Looking

DULL KNIFE——Cheyenne chief who allied with Crazy Horse in 1876

HE DOG——lifelong friend of Crazy Horse who often fought with him

HIGH FOREHEAD——Miniconjou Sioux, prominent in Grattan affair at Fort Laramie in 1854

HORN CHIPS——a *wichasha wakan* who often gave advice to Crazy Horse; also known as Chips or Encouraging Bear

HUMP—Crazy Horse's *kola* (close friend); also known as High Back Bone

ICE—Cheyenne medicine man who shared a close relationship with Crazy Horse. Before the Battle of Solomon River in 1857, he and his associate Dark predicted that soldiers' bullets would not hurt the Sioux warriors.

INKPADUTA—Santee Sioux chief and leader of the Minnesota uprisings during the early 1860s

IRON HAWK—warrior who fought with Crazy Horse

LITTLE CROW—Santee Sioux chief and advocate of peace who turned to war during the Minnesota uprisings of the early 1860s

LITTLE BIG MAN—friend of Crazy Horse and later a member of the Indian Agency police. He restrained Crazy Horse during the skirmish at Camp Robinson in late 1876.

LITTLE HAWK—Crazy Horse's brother

LITTLE THUNDER—Brulé Sioux chief. Crazy Horse was with his band during the Battle of Ash Hollow in 1855.

LONE BEAR—close friend of Crazy Horse who fought with him until his early death in 1866

NO WATER—husband of Black Buffalo woman; enemy of Crazy Horse

OLD MAN AFRAID OF HIS HORSES—Oglala Sioux leader well respected by both Natives and whites; also known as Old Man Afraid

RATTLE BLANKET WOMAN—Crazy Horse's mother

RED CLOUD—Oglala Sioux chief and warrior. He fought the soldiers in Red Cloud's War during the late 1860s and was head of his own agency after the signing of the Fort Laramie treaty in 1868.

RED FEATHER—lifelong friend of Crazy Horse; often fought with him

SITTING BULL—Hunkpapa Sioux chief, *wichasha wakan* and friend of Crazy Horse, who resisted white advances

SPOTTED TAIL—Brulé Sioux chief, uncle of Crazy Horse and head of his own agency after the Fort Laramie treaty of 1868. He advocated peace with the whites.

TOUCH THE CLOUDS—Miniconjou Sioux chief who helped Crazy Horse after his surrender

TWO MOONS—Cheyenne chief. His band was attacked in 1876 by soldiers who thought it was Crazy Horse's band

WOMAN'S DRESS—childhood friend of Crazy Horse who became his enemy; nephew of Red Cloud; also known as Pretty One

YELLOW WOMAN—Cheyenne woman who Crazy Horse rescued after the Battle of Ash Hollow

YOUNG MAN AFRAID OF HIS HORSES—Oglala Sioux chief and son of Old Man Afraid of His Horses; head of Indian Agency police; a friend of Crazy Horse who advocated peace with the whites

WASICHUS (WHITES)

LUCIEN AUGUSTE—translator at Fort Laramie who was assigned to the Grattan command in 1854

FREDERICK BENTEEN—captain under Custer during the Battle of the Little Bighorn in 1876

LUTHER BRADLEY—colonel in command of Camp Robinson near the Red Cloud Agency

DANIEL BURKE—captain and commander of Camp Sheridan near the Spotted Tail Agency

HENRY CARRINGTON—colonel in charge of the Department of the Platte; responsible for constructing forts along the Bozeman Trail in 1866

JOHN CHIVINGTON—colonel of the Colorado Volunteers who led his men in an attack on peaceful Cheyenne in 1864 (Sand Creek Massacre)

WILLIAM CLARK—captain and military commander at Red Cloud Agency near Camp Robinson. Crazy Horse surrendered to him.

PATRICK CONNOR—general in charge of the failed 1865 Powder River Expedition against the Natives

GEORGE CROOK—general in command of the Department of the Platte during the Plains Native battles of the mid- to late 1870s; known to the Sioux as Three Stars

GEORGE ARMSTRONG CUSTER—lieutenant colonel in charge of the Seventh Cavalry; leader of the Black Hills Expedition; defeated at the Battle of the Little Bighorn; known by the Sioux as Long Hair

NEWTON EDMUNDS—governor of Dakota Territory who negotiated the 1865 Fort Sully Treaties

JOHN EVANS—governor of Colorado during the Cheyenne-Arapaho War in the mid-1860s

WILLIAM FETTERMAN—captain assigned by Carrington to relieve woodcutters trapped by the Sioux outside Fort Phil Kearny in 1866. His command was wiped out.

HUGH FLEMMING—second lieutenant in charge of Fort Laramie during the Grattan affair in 1854

JOHN GRATTAN—second lieutenant at Fort Laramie charged with arresting High Forehead, the Miniconjou Sioux who killed a Mormon settler's cow in 1854. His command was wiped out.

FRANK GROUARD—army translator and guide; lived with Crazy Horse for a time but became his enemy

WILLIAM S. HARNEY—brigadier general in charge of the 1855 Sioux Expedition to punish Natives for their defeat of John Grattan; known by the Sioux as the Hornet

JESSE LEE—lieutenant and second in command at Camp Sheridan. He accompanied Crazy Horse to Camp Robinson before his arrest.

VALENTINE MCGILLYCUDDY—doctor at Camp Robinson who treated Crazy Horse after he was attacked there in September 1877

ANSON MILLS—captain under the command of Crook who fought at the battles of the Rosebud and Slim Buttes

NELSON MILES—general in command of northern forces during the Plains wars of the mid- to late 1870s; known by the Sioux as Bear Coat

DAVID MITCHELL—colonel and superintendent of Indian Affairs who negotiated the 1851 Horse Creek Treaty (Fort Laramie Treaty)

ALEXANDER RAMSAY—negotiator for the 1851 Treaty of Mendota with the Santee Sioux in Minnesota; later a governor

MARCUS RENO—major under Custer during the Battle of the Little Bighorn in 1876

BENJAMIN SHAPP—special agent appointed by commissioner of Indian Affairs to investigate matters dealing with Crazy Horse after his surrender

PHILIP SHERIDAN—general and commander of the Department of the Missouri

WILLIAM SHERMAN—general in chief of the United States Army

HENRY SIBLEY—colonel who led troops against hostile Sioux during the Minnesota uprisings of the early 1860s

ALFRED SULLY—general who defeated the Santee Sioux at the Battle of Kildeer Mountain in 1864

EDWIN SUMNER—colonel who defeated the Cheyenne at the Battle of the Solomon River in 1857

E.B. TAYLOR—head of the commission appointed by President Johnson to negotiate with the Sioux in 1865

ALFRED TERRY—commissioner in the negotiations that closed the Bozeman Trail in 1868; commander of the offensive against the northern Sioux in 1876

PROLOGUE

IN EARLY SUMMER 1865, a weary Crazy Horse returned to his Oglala Sioux camp south of the Powder River country. He had been wielding his war club since the Moon of the Dark Red Calves (February) and had joined with his Cheyenne friends to fight the Wasichus (white men) along the South Platte River. Crazy Horse had shared in victories and many successful raids, but he tired of fighting the Wasichus. A man showed little of his worth and ability by exchanging bullets and arrows from a distance, which was the type of warfare usually necessary when fighting the Wasichus. Crazy Horse longed for hand-to-hand combat, where courage counted and bravery was respected. So he had ridden to Crow territory west of the White Mountains (Bighorn Mountains), where he sought out his people's traditional enemies. The Crow knew how to fight.

Eventually, however, it was necessary to return to his band and prepare for the buffalo hunt. As he approached the camp, he noticed that it was more animated than usual. The women were moving around quickly with purpose, and the men were gathered in lively conversation.

"Crazy Horse!"

Crazy Horse looked and saw his brother Little Hawk. The pair embraced.

"You've returned," said Little Hawk. "With many stories of coups counted, I'm certain. Not that I'll ever hear you tell of them." Little Hawk knew of his brother's reluctance to speak of his own deeds.

"When fighting Wasichus, there's little worth saying, little brother," laughed Crazy Horse. "But what goes on here?"

"The Big Bellies have called for a ceremony to install new shirt wearers," replied Little Hawk.

"Ahh," nodded Crazy Horse.

The shirt wearers held a critical position within the rather simple—and effective—system of Sioux governance. Tribal chiefs and headmen, the small group of elders known as the Big Bellies, made decisions on camping positions, warfare and hunting, which usually reflected a consensus of opinion. Their decisions were implemented by the elite warriors known as the shirt wearers, so called because at their investiture they were each given a colored shirt to indicate their position. To be a shirt wearer was to enjoy great prominence in the tribe but the role also carried considerable duties and obligations. Crazy Horse had long desired such a position in his heart.

The importance of the ceremony was quickly evident. A large lodge had been erected in the middle of the camp circle. The smells of cooked buffalo and dog wafted over the camp, and anticipation infused young and old. As the ceremony began, rings of band members circled the center lodge, first warriors, then women and finally children. A select group of warriors, all dressed in their finest apparel, mounted their horses and rode around the camp. They made the circuit three times, on each occasion calling the name of a brave who had been chosen as a shirt wearer. Young Man Afraid of His Horses, Sword and American Horse were selected, each relatives of the Big Bellies. They made a fourth pass and selected Crazy Horse. It was something of a surprise. He had no powerful relatives within the tribe. He commanded no *akicita* (who also enforced band decisions), who he might draw on for support. Crazy Horse knew that he was selected for his ability, to acknowledge his skill and prominence as a warrior.

Hide shirt belonging to Crazy Horse; decorated with paint, scalplocks and woodpecker feathers

When the shirt wearers were gathered near the center lodge, an elder rose and spoke to them of their duties. "You will lead the warriors, both in camp and on the march. You will see that order is preserved and that there is no violence. You must ensure that all Oglala have their rights respected. Be wise, kind and firm in all things. Counsel, advise and then command if necessary. Those who are deaf to your words will rightly feel your strength," he declared as he made a fist. "But they will know that you act out of justice and for the betterment of your people."

The four warriors were then given their shirts, each one sewn from the skins of two bighorn sheep. They were colorful and intricately quilled and fringed with locks of hair, each representing a courageous act of the warrior who had given it. Crazy Horse had more than 240 locks on his shirt.

Another elder rose and spoke directly to the shirt wearers. "Today you are no longer important. You must always think of others first. Look out for the poor, the orphaned, the widowed. If someone harms you, it must be ignored, as is the dog that lifts its leg at your tipi. It will not be easy," he acknowledged, "but you have been chosen because you are great-hearted, generous, strong and brave. I know that you will do your duty gladly and with a big heart."

With that, the celebration began. Crazy Horse wasn't in the mood to join in the high-spirited affair. He was never given to displays of emotion, and he didn't feel comfortable around others who did. On this occasion he had much to think about, and he slipped away. His new position did not bring him material gain, which was irrelevant to Crazy Horse. He was content with his pony and weapons of war. But, at the age of 25, being chosen as a shirt wearer marked him as a great Oglala warrior. It was a matter of satisfaction and a matter of great responsibility.

CHAPTER ONE

A Boy and a Vision

TO THE NORTHEAST of *Paha Sapa* (the Black Hills), cradled by a distant bend in the Belle Fourche River, a steep hill rises unexpectedly from the flat, grassy plains. While its presence is dramatic, little in the butte's appearance suggests that it is special. It is a hill little different from the others that occasionally dot the midwestern plains. Pine trees struggle against the rock and gravel slopes in a losing battle. The trees enjoy greater success upon the broad, flat summit, and they add dashes of dark green and scattered splashes of reddish orange to an otherwise drab grayish brown. The significance of the butte, however, is not in its appearance. The butte is a mysterious place and those who know of its mystery consider it sacred. The Sioux are among that number.*

---

*The name "Sioux" is a corruption of the Chippewa word, meaning "enemy." The Sioux called themselves Oceti Sakowin, the "Seven Council Fires," indicative of their political divisions. These can be divided into three groups: the Santee (Dakota), the Wiciyela (Nakota) and the Teton (Lakota). The Oglala are one of the seven tribes of the Teton Sioux. The Teton lived in the western Dakotas, in eastern Wyoming and Montana and on the southern plains of Canada. They were true Plains people, dependent on the buffalo and nomadic in their lifestyle.

A long time ago, say the Sioux, a young hunter stumbled upon a cave at the base of the butte's eastern slope. The entrance was large enough to easily allow a mature buffalo to pass. As the hunter drew closer, he saw that the rock face around the entrance was decorated with drawings of many different animals. When he finally decided to enter the cave, he found bracelets, pipes and other ornaments scattered on the ground. These objects seemed to be offerings to some powerful spirit. The hunter followed the narrowing cave until he could tell by the distant echo of his footsteps that he was in another large space. It was so dark that he could no longer see his hands, so he hurried back out and returned to his people to tell them what he had seen.

The chief of the village was intrigued by the young hunter's story, but he was not so sure that it was true. He selected four of his bravest warriors to return to the cave with the hunter and investigate the strange place. When they arrived, the hunter noticed that the drawings near the entrance were different than they had been, and he refused to go any farther. The braves, however, were not deterred. Inside the entrance they found the ornaments. They continued on until they reached the large, dark cavern. They put their hands on the walls and felt their way deeper into the cave. The warriors passed through an entrance that was so narrow they had to turn sideways to squeeze through it. They passed through another that was so low they had to crawl. While crawling they came upon a hole from which issued a sweet odor. The pleasant smell stopped them, and they breathed it deeply. After a brief council, they decided it was best to turn back and report their discovery to the chief.

When they reached the room nearest the entrance, one declared, "I am going to take a bracelet to show that we are telling the truth."

"No!" the others replied quickly in unison. "This is the lodge of some Great Spirit and an accident is sure to befall you if you take something that is not yours."

Mato Sapa (Bear Butte), the mountain home of powerful spirits, considered sacred by the Sioux

"You fellows are like old women," he laughed and he slipped a bracelet onto his wrist.

The warriors returned to the village and revealed what they had seen. The warrior with the bracelet held it high for all to see. None doubted that the butte was indeed home to powerful spirits.

Some days later, the four warriors were setting traps for wolves. The traps consisted of heavy logs supported by sticks. Each man dug a hole near a stick and placed a piece of meat a few feet away from the hole. They surrounded the meat with willow boughs so that the wolf would have to push his way into the hole to get it. In so doing, the wolf would knock the stick out and become trapped under the log. As the warrior with the bracelet prepared his trap, he knocked the stick away and caught his wrist under the log. The pain was intense, and he gasped sharply. When his friends finally released him, his wrist was broken.

"You have been punished for taking the bracelet out of the mysterious butte," they told him.

He thought they spoke the truth.

The Sioux knew powerful spirits dwelt at the butte, but they did not know if they were good or evil. Some time after the accident, another young man went to the butte. He found the cave and his eyes fixed on the drawings beside the entrance. He saw a drawing of a woman gripping a sturdy pole that held a large amount of venison. Another pole nearby was broken in two pieces, apparently from the weight of the meat. Around the drawings were the marks of many buffalo hooves. When his eyes fell to the ground, he saw the hoofprints of the animal scattered there also.

The young man returned hurriedly to the village to tell what he had seen. Everyone was excited but no one knew what the drawings might mean. It was made clear the next day when a great herd of buffalo appeared near the village. The warriors killed many animals, and the villagers laughed while they worked, trying hard to remember when they had last enjoyed such a successful hunt. One woman was holding meat on a long pole that snapped unexpectedly under the weight. She took a stronger tent pole that might better support the many strips of meat. The young man saw her and realized that it was just as he had seen in the drawing. The spirits at the mysterious butte had revealed themselves as helpful to the Sioux.

Ever after the people traveled regularly to the butte to seek direction in the drawings left by the powerful spirits. It was truly a sacred place, and many Sioux believed that the butte was the prophet of the people.

~~~~~

In the fall of 1840, a Hunkpatila band of Oglala Sioux made its way to the mysterious butte of Sioux legend in present-day west-central South Dakota. The journey from the heavily treed shores of the Powder River across the plains west of *Paha Sapa* to the butte that rose to the northeast of those hills was familiar. The band had made the trip each year for many years. The Oglala was one of the seven tribes of the Teton Sioux that gathered at the butte to hold councils and to perform rituals under the watchful eyes of the powerful spirits who dwelt in the caves. When the Hunkpatila arrived, they found that many other Sioux were already camped at the foot of the butte. Their presence was cause for excitement because it meant that there would be many stories of adventure and bravery to hear and old acquaintances to renew. The Hunkpatila band made its way to the camp of the Bad Faces Oglala, with whom they usually associated, and set up their lodges.

The Hunkpatila band was not large; the Oglala were known for camping in small groups. Among their number were Crazy Horse and his wife Rattle Blanket Woman. Crazy Horse was an Oglala who was respected among his people as a *wichasha wakan*, a holy man. Rattle Blanket Woman was a Miniconjou Sioux, and she counted among her family leaders of that tribe. They had been married for a few years, and Rattle Blanket Woman was heavy with the couple's second child. They were not camped long when she slipped away from the great circle of lodges to a secluded area where she gave birth to a boy.

The elderly woman who assisted her delivery gasped when she saw the infant. Rattle Blanket Woman's eyes grew large in concern, and she understood the old woman's anxiety when her son was placed in her arms.

Rattle Blanket Woman wrapped the infant's lower part in moss, swaddled him in soft doeskin and secured him in a cradleboard that she slipped onto her back. Then, weak though she was, Rattle Blanket Woman returned quickly to her lodge, where she found an anxious Crazy Horse waiting.

Crazy Horse could see by the look on his wife's face that something was wrong. He listened for the infant's cry but heard nothing.

"Is the baby well?"

"Your son is fine," she replied.

Crazy Horse smiled. To be blessed with a son, a hunter and warrior-to-be, was a great thing.

"But you say it without enthusiasm," he observed. "What is the matter?"

Rattle Blanket Woman lifted the cradleboard from her back and took the infant from it.

"See for yourself," she suggested.

Crazy Horse took the infant in his hands and held him before the lodge fire. Uncertain that the flickering of the fire was deceiving him, he stepped from the lodge into the sunlight.

"His skin is the light color of the Wasichu (white man)!" he muttered in disbelief. "His hair, too. It is not dark and straight, but sandy and curly."

"What can this mean, husband?" asked Rattle Blanket Woman, who had followed him outside.

Crazy Horse raised his eyebrows and widened his eyes. "I do not know," he replied as he shook his head gently. "But perhaps I can find out."

Later that night under a full moon, Crazy Horse climbed the gradual eastern slope of the butte. He went there in search of a vision. Any Sioux might be granted a vision, but what a *wichasha wakan* saw was special. Such a man enjoyed a unique relationship with the spirits, a relationship that endowed him with great power. A *wichasha wakan* possessed the gift of prophecy. In his visions he was granted a glimpse of what was to be.

Reaching the flat summit of the butte, Crazy Horse performed the secret rituals of a *wichasha wakan*. Seated, he smoked his pipe, hopeful that his prayers for guidance would be carried to Wakan Tanka, the Great Mystery, in the small clouds of rising smoke. The tobacco spent, he stood, looked up to the sky and sang. He did so until the moon slipped into its lodge and the sun woke from its place of sleep far beyond the eastern plains. Somber-faced, he returned to the camp below.

He was not there long when he sent word to the chiefs and head-men of the gathered bands. He wanted a council because he had something important to say. None hesitated when a *wichasha wakan* called for a council, and that night a great gathering was held in the council lodge. News of Crazy Horse's son had spread throughout the camp, and everyone wondered whether his words would explain the infant's strange features. As they sat waiting, Crazy Horse filled the ceremonial pipe and lit it with a glowing buffalo chip he had placed at the fire's edge. He held the stem towards the earth so that it might hold the people well. He presented the bowl to each of the four winds so that they might not blow cruelly. Finally, he held the pipe towards the sun so that it might light their way. Then Crazy Horse passed it around the circle from right to left in the direction of the sun's journey. Each of the chiefs and the headmen inhaled deeply, and when the pipe returned to Crazy Horse, he spoke.

"Last night Wakan Tanka appeared to me in the form of a bear. He bestowed upon me powers to conquer all earthly beings, including the Wasichus who are coming into our land. They are not yet here in great numbers, but I have seen them darken the plains as the buffalo do. But I am not a warrior, so I wondered if this gift was meant for me? No, I concluded. The gift was given to me, but I am not the one to use it. I give the gift to my son, who will grow strong. He will use the gift of the bear spirit to become a greater leader of our people."

Crazy Horse's words were met with silence. What was there to say? No one dreamed that there could ever be so many Wasichus, but then again none had the dreams of a *wichasha wakan*. It also seemed unlikely that one who looked so much like the Wasichus would offer protection from them. The band had much to consider, and even as they went their separate ways some weeks later, most were still thinking about the sandy-haired, light-skinned boy, Crazy Horse's vision and the mysterious powers of what all were calling *Mato Sapa* (Bear Butte).

The boy who was named Light Hair, but was called Curly, knew nothing of his father's vision. He would not be burdened with the singular responsibility of his future, and any effort to lead him in that direction would have been considered unseemly by a people who treasured a person's freedom to choose a life path. All his family and people could do was ensure that the boy was raised properly so that he might be ready when the time came to fulfill the vision. As a result, Curly was reared in the manner of other Sioux boys.

From his first days, he learned of the importance of community among his people, and he grew secure with the sense of belonging. His maternal female relatives were all mothers to him, just as his paternal male relatives were all fathers to him. The elderly, regardless of relation, were his grandparents. When he was liberated from the cradleboard at about the age of two and allowed to roam the camp as he saw fit, Curly learned that every lodge was open to him and that he might stop for food or play without fear of chastisement. It was a warm feeling, a good feeling.

But Curly was not to enjoy a childhood free from tragedy. At the age of four, He Crow, Crazy Horse's younger brother, was killed while leading a disastrous raid against the Crow. Rattle Blanket Woman was especially fond of her brother-in-law and her grief upon learning of his death was overwhelming. Despondent, she hanged herself from a tree. Curly understood little except that his mother was gone. Crazy Horse soon remarried, taking two sisters, siblings of the powerful Brulé Sioux chief Spotted Tail. One of them bore him a son in 1846, who would be known as Little Hawk. Curly grew close to his brother, but losing his mother coupled with the loss of the sense of security that should have come from that bond was to affect him profoundly.

At his young age, however, the loss was mostly forgotten in the carefree life of a Sioux boy. Boys had great freedom and could do much as they liked. For a time, boys were content to sit and mimic the domesticity of adults, but soon such mundane activities could not contain their energy, they began running throughout the camp, chasing dogs and each other in turn. At most, a villager who could no longer endure the shouting and barking around his lodge might remind the boys that the owl, a much-feared creature, would take them away if they didn't settle down.

Such reminders were few because the boys' activities increasingly took them away from the village. By ages six or seven they were playing the war games that came to dominate their young lives. "Throw the Mud" had the boys dividing into sides and attacking each other with mud balls propelled from the end of springy willow sticks. When the game was done, they'd scrub the mud off in a stream, although long afternoons or evenings spent in the water suggested that they considered cleanup to be something less than a chore.

"Fighting the Bee Tribe" involved greater preparation and risk. As the boys painted their faces, they imagined that a nearby bee's nest was a band of Crow warriors, traditional enemies of the Sioux. Quietly and cautiously, they approached the nest until, with a war whoop, they launched their attack. But Curly suspected that the Bee tribe was unlike any Native enemy because they were always prepared, and the boys would have to run for the nearest stream to avoid their stings. Those who fell victim to the bees were not allowed to participate in the mock scalp dance that followed, an exclusion that was most embarrassing.

The games of early childhood were not pedantic in any way, but they were important educational tools because they socialized children into the world of the Sioux. Eventually, direction was introduced into the activities of childhood. Little is known of Curly's experiences during this period of his life, but an uncle usually shouldered the educational responsibilities for a boy. His uncle likely gave him his first set of bow and arrows, and perhaps some cursory instruction, but it was up to Curly to master its use with long and determined practice. Encouragement was rarely needed because boys knew that a man's reputation rested on his ability to hunt and raid, both of which required skill with the bow and arrow. Soon stationary targets were replaced with squirrels and rabbits. Success was evident in the full pots simmering over lodge fires and in the smiles and kind words of villagers.

Curly's education was wide-ranging. His uncle shared myth stories about the Sioux, few of which were new to Curly as he had heard them since infancy. But these stories were important because they explained Sioux origins, outlined proper conduct and ensured that the younger generation realized that the past lived in the present. Occasionally, Curly's uncle also told of his own personal experiences, particularly those that revealed a lesson about what it meant to be a warrior or hunter. Other times the lesson was more explicit, as when Curly was wakened with a war whoop before the sun appeared from its lodge or challenged to a day of fasting. Such activities taught Curly the importance of preparation and fortitude.

Great emphasis was placed on honing Curly's observation skills because survival depended on an intimate knowledge of nature. Every day that Curly and his uncle were together began with the same command, "Look twice at what is around you." Wherever they traveled, Curly described what he saw and tried to draw conclusions from it. A small hole in dense brush indicated a rabbit run and a meal in a time of need. A bird with a muddy beak revealed a nearby source of water. A heavy growth of moss on the side of a tree showed the locations of the four winds' lodges. It was important that Curly remember such things because at the end of the day he was always questioned about what he had seen. He was an attentive pupil, and such practices ensured that he grew wise to the ways of the world around him.

While community was important to the Sioux, a warrior was ultimately dependent on himself and on the goodwill of Wakan Tanka. Curly couldn't learn everything a Sioux boy was expected to know in the company of others. Many days found him unaccompanied in the woods or on the plains thinking about what his uncle had told him or testing his memory as he surveyed his surroundings. As he wandered alone, he began to get a measure of himself, to understand and conquer his body and to recognize and confront his fears. Curly did not need encouragement to set off on his own. He enjoyed the solitude because he felt that he did not really fit in with his peers. By nature he was reserved, and his light complexion heightened his unease among others. Perhaps he might have adjusted more easily had he not been deprived of a close relationship with his mother and the special sense of security that the bond provided.

It may have been on one of his solitary journeys that Curly made the resolution that was to shape his life. He decided to dedicate himself to becoming a warrior, to make a reputation as a great one. Perhaps he thought that such renown might ease the pain of being different from others. He knew from his uncle that the warrior's path was long and difficult. While most Sioux boys aspired to travel the path, his uncle had explained to him that it was not easily traveled. To be a warrior meant possessing the four great virtues of the Sioux—bravery, generosity, fortitude and wisdom. These virtues were learned over a lifetime, and for many, even that was not long enough. Curly was determined to be prepared, so that when opportunities appeared on his path he would be able to make the best choices, the ones that led to warriorhood.

~~~~~

In the spring of 1851 Curly's Hunkpatila band traveled south to the fork of the Platte River where they joined with Old Smoke's band of Bad Faces Oglala. The band would do some trading and hunt buffalo before they made their way north again in late summer. Occasionally, they stayed longer than necessary into the Moon of the Changing Season (September). Most laughed and said it was because Old Smoke had a sweet tooth that found relief in the goods available from Jim Bordeaux and other local traders.

Curly didn't see much of the traders because they operated farther west along the North Platte River, near Fort Laramie. Curly had learned that it was best to stay away from the territory near the fort. Bull Bear, chief of the Walks as She Thinks Oglala band, was camped there, and he was an enemy of Old Smoke. Any friend of the Bad Faces was likely to meet with trouble if he ventured near Bull Bear's camp. Natives who had grown dependent on the trade goods and handouts of the Wasichus also surrounded the fort. Natives who pursued traditional ways scorned the Laramie Loafers, as those living around the fort were called.

Curly didn't much care for the Laramie Loafers, but it was the Wasichus around the fort that troubled him most. He went to Fort Laramie once with his father, and the Wasichus had pointed at him. He heard them speak as they did so, although he didn't understand what they said. It was just as well because he would not have liked their words. They had noticed his light skin and wondered whether he was a captive.

But Curly still saw plenty of Wasichus because many of them traveled the trail that followed the North Platte River. He rarely saw them up north so he often took time to watch them. On this day he lay hidden in the high grass that rolled back from the river's shore and stared across the water at the long line of Wasichus. He had been observing them since the sun was high in the sky, and even as the shadows grew long he knew more were coming. In the east he could see the clouds of dust their animals kicked up.

"Taking a nap, Curly?"

Curly's head snapped up, and he looked to his side. It was High Backbone, known as Hump. He was a Miniconjou Sioux, a few years older than Curly. They had met in the spring, when Hump's band had joined with Curly's. Over the summer they had become good friends. He would eventually become Curly's *kola*, a close friend with whom he partnered in all activities and to whom he pledged to share his takings on raids and in hunts.

"I knew you were there," replied Curly, defensively.

"Uh-huh," said Hump, unconvinced.

"There are many Wasichus," observed Curly, anxious to change the subject. "Their line has not been broken this day."

"Their tribe must be large," suggested Hump. "I cannot remember coming to Fort Laramie without seeing the Holy Road choked with them." The Holy Road was the name the Sioux had given to the trail used by the western-bound Wasichus. Since soldiers arrived with their rifles, Natives dared not harm them.

"I am glad to see them continue west," said Curly.

The boys remained silent for a while. Eventually, Hump proposed a race back to the village and they were off.

Fort Laramie had been built in the mid-1830s as a trading post. The army purchased the fort in 1849, but it never quite shed its trading origins, and it attracted many Plains Natives eager to barter for supplies. The army's interest in the fort was strategic. They used it as a base to protect overland migrants traveling west on the California/Oregon Trail (the Holy Road) , which was, by the late 1840s, the preferred route west for countless covered wagons, whose thousands of passengers had their eyes set on new beginnings on the American frontier.

Every immigrant had his or her own reason for setting out from Independence, Kansas, or Nebraska City on the Missouri River. Usually their reasons became clear at Fort Bridger, southwest of the

Fort Laramie in the late 1850s with a Sioux encampment in the foreground. The fort was built in 1834 by the fur trader William Sublette and originally called Fort William in his honor. In the years that followed, the fort became increasingly popular with the many western-bound settlers traveling the California/Oregon Trail. In 1849 the United States government purchased the fort and turned it into a military post. While the soldiers protected the settlers, Fort Laramie continued as the main commercial post east of the Rocky Mountains. Fort Laramie was also in the southern range of traditional Sioux territory, so the Sioux traded there. Some became dependent on the fort and were derisively called the Laramie Loafers by Crazy Horse and others. Major treaties were made in the vicinity of the fort in 1851 and 1868.

Sweetwater River in the Rocky Mountains, where the trail forked. Those who had their eyes set on fortune continued west along the California Trail to the gold fields. Others sought a more certain future, heading northwest along the Oregon Trail to the rich farmland of the Oregon Territory. Some weren't pulled west so much as they were pushed from the east. They desired freedom from the constraints of eastern society, from others telling them what to think and how to behave. All sought an opportunity where people could gain true measures of themselves as they carved out homes and communities.

But getting there was a challenge because the California/Oregon Trail cut through southern Teton Sioux territory. Agreements of goodwill had been made between government officials and the Sioux in the 1830s. For an annual payment, the Sioux let the settlers travel west unmolested. The Sioux weren't much interested in the Wasichus at this time. They were busy fighting Crow, Pawnee and other traditional enemies, and the little interaction they had with settlers was mostly positive. The Natives provided game, fish and firewood. They loaned the Wasichus their horses and helped pull wagons over difficult terrain. They even worked as guides. In those early days, their provisions and services were often given free of charge, but the Sioux soon learned that they could make money, and migrants regularly reported their surprise at the shrewdness of Native bargaining.

Throughout the mid- to late 1840s, the relationship soured. Settlers grumbled that Natives were stealing their supplies. Reports of war parties that rode to attack Native enemies further frayed the nerves of settlers who feared they were also about to be attacked. Natives grumbled among themselves and complained to traders and soldiers that the Wasichus were dividing the buffalo herd and scaring off game. Their animals ate too much grass, leaving little for wild game. Cholera epidemics, unknown before the arrival of the Wasichus, ravaged the Native population. Soon, angry words became violence. Killings were few, and more Natives than settlers died, but the bloodshed was troublesome. By the late 1840s, events pressured the United States government to make treaty with the Plains tribes. In 1851, Superintendent of Indian Affairs Colonel David Mitchell was dispatched to Fort Laramie with orders to bring peace to the territory along the California/Oregon Trail.

Mitchell's task was challenging. The Crow, Shoshone and Pawnee, enemies of the Sioux, were reluctant to travel to the council because it was in Sioux territory. Mitchell assured them that there would be no violence, but the Pawnee didn't come. Eventually, eight tribes were represented, including the Cheyenne, Arapaho and most of the Sioux tribes. By August, 10,000 Natives had gathered around Fort Laramie. Within weeks, they had exhausted all the available grass and game. Mitchell, aware that supplies to provision the Natives would be late in arriving and fearful that hunger might bring about unrest, asked the tribes to relocate to a more suitable site. By early September, the Natives had moved 30 miles downstream to Horse Creek, a tributary of the North Platte.

Curly thought the gathering at the treaty grounds a wondrous sight. He had never seen so many Natives in one place before. Few had. He could walk for a day and still not make his way around the camp! He watched wide-eyed as a company of Wasichu dragoons, so well dressed and disciplined, assembled outside Mitchell's tent. With pride, he saw that the Sioux chiefs and headmen were also dressed in their finest attire, although he also noticed that some members of the eastern tribes were dirty and wore ragged clothing. He knew that they lived closer to the land of the Wasichu, and he suspected that proximity had something to do with their condition.

Curly glanced up at the sun and saw it was high in the sky. He quickly forgot about the council as he ran for his pony. A game of "Throwing-Them-Off-Their-Horses" had been organized, and Curly was keen to participate. While the games played up north were fun, the small number of boys in a Hunkpatila winter camp provided a poor stick against which to measure ability. At Horse Creek, Curly discovered that games and competitions took on new meaning because of the many boys against whom he could test his skills. He set about doing so with dogged determination, always giving his greatest effort.

When he did, he expected to be the best, but that was not usually the case when the competition included older boys. Curly's strength did not yet match his desire, and this sometimes placed him in difficult situations. Once on a dare, Curly climbed onto the back of a buffalo calf. He discovered that he could not bring it to a halt and had to hold on tight until the animal tired. The episode brought much laughter, but Curly could not say "No" to a dare. Doing what the older boys asked was a way to ease his feelings of shyness and awkwardness. Even when he was not quite successful, making an effort brought a degree of comfort mostly unfamiliar to Curly.

Curly hurried to the field just north of the camp, where most of the boys were already gathered. Choosing teams was not necessary on this occasion because boys joined with their fellow band members. Honor was on the line in this game! Curly spotted the Hunkpatila and made his way to them. He found his brother Little Hawk there.

"Brother, you are too young for this game," said Curly. "You have not yet the strength and are sure to be quickly thrown from your horse."

"But I am fast, brother," replied Little Hawk.

"Yes," agreed Curly. "The rabbit, too, is fast, but when the bear gets hold of him, his speed no longer matters. There are bears in this game, and they will get hold of you. Best you watch this time. I do not want to take a broken rabbit back to Father."

Little Hawk's shoulders sagged, but he knew the dangers of "Throwing-Them-Off-Their-Horses." It was a real battle in all but the killing. Even the biggest boys were sometimes hurt. Little Hawk obeyed his brother and rode to the side. Curly's band formed a line.

To their sides and across the field were lines of boys from other bands. Curly saw teams from all the Sioux tribes. There, down the line among the Miniconjou, was Hump. Curly caught his eye and smiled. A shout signaled that the game was on.

The boys charged each other with great force, their ponies rearing up at the last second before contact. Amidst the war whoops and dust, each boy lunged for an opponent in an effort to dismount him. Boys who fell to the ground were considered dead. After a few minutes, the boys who were still on their horses reassembled. They waited while their fallen comrades made their way to the side, some of them limping, holding their sides or rubbing their heads. A further delay occurred as others on the ground wrestled. It wasn't quite according to the rules, but blood was hot and tempers flared. With another shout, they were off again.

The game continued until the number was reduced to less than 10, and only two bands were represented. Curly and the Hunkpatila were among their number. A final charge would decide the victor. Curly rode hard. He was an excellent rider with an unusual number of years of experience for one so young because his father had given him a horse when he was five. But his riding skills were not enough on this occasion. He tried to drive his pony past an opponent, make a quick turn and strike. But as he slipped past, the other boy yanked on Curly's bridle, causing the head of his horse to pull up unexpectedly. Curly was hit flush on the chest by the animal's neck and thrown to the ground. To add injury to the indignity, he rolled into a bed of stinging nettles. He tried not to wince, but Hump, also out of the game, saw his pain. He waited for Curly to return to the side.

"Come," said Hump, as he put his hand on Curly's back. "Let me help you."

Curly looked at him for a moment and decided to accept his friend's offer. The two left the playing field and made their way towards the river.

"Swim," advised Hump. "The cool water will make the skin tight and the stingers easier to remove."

Curly took off his breechcloth and made his way into the river. Soon he was lying on his stomach, and Hump was carefully pulling out the stingers.

"Have you heard anything about the great council?" asked Curly.

"The Wasichus want our people to chose a single man to speak for us," replied Hump, who had heard the braves talking.

"What does that mean, 'to speak for us'?"

"They want a chief whose words bind us all."

"All the Sioux?"

"Yes."

"I do not understand that. How can one man speak for all?" asked Curly.

"He can't, yet that is what the Wasichus demand. And they want more," added Hump. "They want us to stop fighting the Crow and Pawnee."

"What!" exclaimed Curly, sitting up suddenly, his pain forgotten. "No more raiding?" This was devastating news. A warrior made his reputation by demonstrating courage and skill while raiding. "It cannot be!"

"Don't worry, brother," advised Hump, who, after a summer together, knew something of Curly's dreams. "I hear that it is what the Wasichu want. Whether they will get it is another matter." He placed his hand on Curly's shoulder. "Now lie back and let me finish."

The treaty negotiations at Horse Creek were unfolding just as Hump had said. Mitchell's first demand was that the Sioux choose someone who could represent all their people, a concept alien to the Sioux. They had no notion of a supreme ruler, no thought that they could give their unquestioned allegiance to one man who would make decisions for everyone. But that was the way in Mitchell's world, and when the Natives could not agree on a man, Mitchell chose the Brulé Conquering Bear. He was respected

A 1930 drawing by William Henry Jackson of the California/Oregon Trail. The route hugged the southern banks of the North Platte River. Although it was just south of traditional Oglala territory, it was close enough for them to see the Wasichus journey west. Throughout the early 1840s, not many white settlers ventured west, but the promise of good land in Oregon and the discovery of gold at Sutter's Mill in California brought them in unimaginable numbers. By the early 1850s, tens of thousands overlanders had passed through Fort Laramie.

among the Sioux, so no one complained, but no one took seriously that the paper chief was their leader.

While most Sioux could live with the strange leadership demand, others opposed Mitchell's request that the Natives cease intertribal warfare. Mitchell's goal was to reduce dangers for travelers on the California/Oregon Trail, but the Sioux saw the request as a blow to their very way of life. Curly was not wrong when he noted that warriors made their reputation by fighting enemies. Some bands, including the Hunkpapa, refused to make treaty for this very reason. Others touched the pen, and in doing so, agreed to the safe passage of settlers, to permit the construction of roads and to live within specified areas. Sioux territory was roughly bounded by the White Earth, Heart, Missouri and Platte rivers, including the Black Hills. The Natives also ceded territory in present-day Montana, Wyoming and North Dakota. For this, they received annuity payments of $50,000 for 50 years. The United States Senate later reduced the term to 10 years, but didn't inform the Natives.

Curly need not have worried about demands regarding intertribal raiding. When the Horse Creek council ended on September 17, the bands returned to their winter camps and continued to raid as they always had. Ultimately, few bands ratified the Horse Creek Treaty of 1851 (also called the 1851 Fort Laramie Treaty).

〜〜〜〜

Hump's Miniconjou and a few other Oglala bands joined Curly's band on the journey north from the Holy Road. They set up camp northeast of the Sand Hills (in present-day southwestern Nebraska), just above the Running Water (Niobrara River). It was a good place to hunt buffalo. They would remain there until their parfleches were full, perhaps until the cold wind blew from the north during the Moon of Falling Leaves (November). It would require much work, and it was made easier and more enjoyable in larger numbers.

Nothing was as important to the Sioux as the buffalo, the animal that Wakan Tanka had created for their sustenance. Its meat provided food, its hide warmth and shelter, its sinews and bones equipment, its blood paint and its dung fuel. But the buffalo was more than a source of provisions. A man showed his skill and bravery during the hunt. Success in the hunt demonstrated that he could support a family. The buffalo was also a sacred animal that served as the foundation for much of the Sioux's spiritual and ceremonial life. The appropriate rituals for those ceremonies had been delivered by Ptesan-Wi, the White Buffalo Woman, a mystical buffalo sent by Wakan Tanka in the form of a woman. The stories of White Buffalo Woman formed the core of Sioux morality, and every Sioux knew them from infancy. The elders sometimes told the tale of her first arrival before a hunt, perhaps hoping that she might bring large buffalo herds.

Curly sat near the lodge fire, one of many children who encircled the crackling flames. Across from the lodge's entrance, in the place of greatest honor, sat grandfather. He filled his pipe with a mixture of tobacco and red willow bark and lit it with the end of a glowing twig. After a few puffs, he placed the pipe in his lap and began to speak.

"A long time ago, before the Oglala had horses, the seven council fires came together and camped. Although it was summer and animals should have been plentiful, none could be found. Search as they might, the scouts always returned with bad news."

Curly knew how serious that was.

"One day, the scouts climbed to the peak of a hill. Able to see far into the distance, they hoped to spot game. They were disappointed. They were about to return to camp when one of the braves called that he saw something. It was far away, and they had to squint to determine what it was. They saw a person. As the figure drew nearer, they could see that it wasn't just any person. Instead of walking, the being floated. The person was holy," explained the grandfather.

"Soon the braves realized that the figure was a woman. Her beauty was greater than ever seen by any of the men. Her long, shiny blue-black hair fell straight near two red dots on her face. Her dark eyes suggested an unknown power. She was dressed in a white buckskin outfit, so white that it glowed in the midday sun. Her clothes were decorated with colorful designs of porcupine quills with an intricacy well beyond the ability of Sioux women. In her hands she carried a large bundle.

"When she arrived at the hilltop, one of the scouts was so taken by her beauty that he reached out to touch her. Immediately, a cloud descended upon him, and snakes devoured his flesh. Only his white bones remained on the ground. The others properly remained still.

" 'I am Ptesan-Wi, and I bring something good for your people,' she said. 'Go back and tell your chief to set up a medicine lodge and to make it holy for my arrival.'

"The scouts returned to camp, and the preparations were made. When Ptesan-Wi arrived, the chief spoke. 'Sister, we are glad you have come to teach us.'

"Pleased, Ptesan-Wi accepted his invitation into the medicine tent. Once there, she opened the bundle. It held the *chanunpa*, the sacred calf pipe. She raised it before those in the tipi, grasping the stem with her right hand and the bowl with her left. It has been held that way ever since," informed the grandfather.

"Ptesan-Wi told the Teton of the importance of the pipe. 'The red bowl is from *Paha Sapa* (the Black Hills). The stone from which it is made is red from the blood of your ancestors. It represents your own flesh. The bowl also represents the buffalo, the sacred animal created by Wakan Tanka to hold back the great waters of the sun's descent. Look closely and you will see seven circles engraved on it. They represent the seven campfires of the Teton. The stem represents everything that grows on the earth. The 12 feathers that hang from it are from Wanblee Galeshka, the eagle, a wise and sacred bird who is Wakan Tanka's messenger.'

" 'The skull and backbone of the *chanunpa* form a living being. When you smoke the *chan-sahsa*, the red willow bark, it creates the breath of Tunkashila, the Great Grandfather Mystery.' As she said this, Ptesan-Wi placed a dry buffalo chip on the fire. When it glowed red, she took it in her hand and lit the pipe. Soon smoke drifted skyward. 'Use the *chanunpa* when you wish to communicate with Wakan Tanka.'

"Ptesan-Wi stood. 'Use the *chanunpa* wisely,' she cautioned. 'Respect it and it will lead you to where you must go. I will see you again.' With that she slipped out of the tent. Once outside of camp, she turned into a buffalo and disappeared. The plains in the distance were suddenly dark with buffalo.

"Ptesan-Wi was true to her word. She returned many times to tell the Teton what was good and necessary, and of the ceremonies that we must perform to show respect to Wakan Tanka and to the created world," concluded the grandfather.

Perhaps Wakan Tanka heard the elder's story because the next day the scouts returned with news of a great buffalo herd. Curly jumped on his horse to join with the hunters, even though he had not yet made his first kill. He watched with envy as Hump gathered his bow and arrows. He had made his first kill a few winters before. Curly longed to make his first kill, an important step on the path to manhood. As yet he only helped the hunters, usually by tending to the ponies at night. The hunt went well, and many buffalo were killed. Dressing the animals was women's work, and with the excitement of the hunt subsiding, Curly and his friends returned to the village. They quickly began a game of "Buffalo Hunt" where all of the boys could pretend they were the hunters they so longed to be.

"Curly, you make too easy a target!" Red Feather shouted, as Curly tried to move a cactus, so that it would be more difficult for an arrow to pass through the hole cut in it. Suddenly, one did.

"Aha! I have pierced the heart of the buffalo!" came an enthusiastic cry. The words weren't even out of his mouth before he was running away with Curly in pursuit. It wasn't much of a chase because Curly was fast. Soon he was poking the hunter in the buttocks with the cactus.

"Enough! Enough!" cried the marksman.

"Yes, it is enough," called He Dog. "Look! The women return with the meat!"

Making its way slowly towards the camp was a line of hunting horses, each laden with buffalo meat. There would be a great feast this night but the impulsive boys could not wait. They rushed over to the horses and gorged themselves on raw liver. The adults smiled. As he ate his fill, Curly thought of the day when he would be old enough to leave the games of childhood behind him. Soon, their bellies round and their faces and hands deep red, the boys left and made for the edge of the camp, where they prepared to wage mock battle against the band. They built grass tipis and waited for their adviser, an older Oglala who provided direction and counsel for the boys. The full moon had replaced the sun, and the noise of the camp's merriment rolled across the plains when Running Bear arrived to help them plan their raiding strategy.

"Listen to them feasting. It is not right that we should sit here while they celebrate. Let us take their meat, so that we may also feast," declared Running Bear. He held out a stick. "Each take a bite. The bigger the piece that you split off, the bigger the piece of meat that you must raid."

Curly waited impatiently for his turn, eager to begin the raid. Finally, he clenched the stick between his teeth and snapped it in half.

"We will eat well tonight," laughed Running Bear, "if Curly's cunning is any match for his mouth."

Curly smiled awkwardly, determined that it would be so. Taking no chances, he was on his belly well before he reached the camp. He crawled to the drying racks, took a long strip of buffalo meat and slowly made his way back to the boys. He was greeted with a cheer. Eventually, all the boys returned, some without meat and with their heads low. They ate little in the feast that followed.

"Our success demands a celebration," declared Running Bear.

"It is time for the chapped breast dance. Whose chest is sunburned the worst?"

The boys didn't have to look far; they all knew it was Curly. His light skin was always redder than the tanned bodies of his friends. As he listened to the other boys call his name, he was glad that it was too dark for anyone to see the embarrassment that reddened his face to an even deeper hue than his chest. But he could not escape what had to be done.

Curly began to dance to the chanting of the other boys, "I have a chapped breast. My breast is red. My breast is yellow."

The words echoed in his mind even as he fell asleep later that night. They might have dominated his thoughts the next day had his father not spoken to him soon after he got up.

"Curly, you have a fast pony?" asked Crazy Horse.

"Yes, father," he replied.

"You have a stout bow and quick arrows?"

"Always, father."

"Then let us go shoot tipis."

Curly's face lit up with a smile rarely seen. Finally, he was going to hunt buffalo! It was a great moment in a boy's life. As soon as they mounted their ponies, Crazy Horse let Curly take the lead. He scouted out the animals, which wasn't difficult since they had not moved too far away. Curly ensured that they approached the herd downwind, so as to give no hint of a human presence. When the pair was close enough, Curly unleashed an arrow. He did not yet have the strength of the older men, whose arrow might pass right through the animal if it did not strike bone. Still, Curly's arrow sank deep into the buffalo's chest, quickly bringing down the bellowing animal. At that moment, Crazy Horse's smile was as big as his son's had been. Curly was a hunter, and suddenly everything seemed possible.

On returning to camp, Curly scouted out Hump so that he could share his triumph with his close friend. Curly found him among a group of boys. He motioned to Hump to draw him away from the others. Hump knew something was up.

"You look like the fox who has eaten a meal he did not catch," said Hump.

"No. I killed my meal, brother," replied Curly.

"A rabbit's not much of a meal," suggested Hump. He suspected that Curly had killed a buffalo, but he felt a little needling was appropriate.

"And it's not only my meal. Today my arrow brought down my first buffalo!"

Hump put his arm around Curly's shoulders.

"The rabbits are safe then!" he laughed. Curly smiled. "Some of the older boys are riding to capture wild horses. Join us."

Curly did not think twice about the invitation.

"I'm ready." He would do anything to be with the older boys.

The horse was important to the Sioux way of life, as it had been since its introduction in the previous century, but the Sioux didn't breed their own horses, preferring to steal them from other tribes or to capture them wild. Stealing horses was the business of warriors, but boys could try to capture the wild ones. Few succeeded, however, because the speed and wiles of the free-spirited animals challenged even the most skilled men. They found a herd near the Sand Hills, and the boys pursued the horses until the animals tired.

When Curly saw his opportunity, he acted quickly. He carried a long willow stick, with a rawhide loop secured by thin buckskin strips to the far end. When he drew near to one of the animals, he slipped the loop over the horse's neck and gave a sharp tug. The rawhide loop broke free and tightened around the animal's neck. Curly urged his mount closer to the wild horse and, once abreast, leaped onto the animal. He held tight through the first turbulent moments as it struggled to break free. Eventually it staggered to the ground, the rawhide loop serving as a noose that cut off its air.

Sioux warriors on horseback in a posed photo taken in 1905.

Curly slipped a rope halter around its neck and strung a connecting rope back between its legs, which he tied to his own horse. When the wild animal jumped up and sought to break free, it pulled against its own nose and, thoroughly confused, soon gave up.

The capture was a moment of pride for Curly, although he did not reveal his pleasure. Hump, however, gave him a knowing smile.

None of his friends nor his brother Little Hawk had yet broken a wild horse. It was an act that his father considered to be of particular importance. On returning to the village, Crazy Horse gave Curly a new name, bestowed to mark a special achievement as was traditional among the Sioux. He was called His Horse Looking. Most in the village, however, continued to call him Curly.

CHAPTER TWO

Troubles along the Platte

HIGH FOREHEAD, A Miniconjou Sioux, sat on the northern bank of the North Platte River trying to ignore the rumbling in his stomach. Even the oppressive heat of the Moon of Black Cherries (August) was forgotten as he rubbed his stomach hard, hoping that the pressure of his hand might shrink his belly and make it feel less empty. He was hungry so often these days that he'd almost grown used to the pangs. He looked west to nearby Fort Laramie, wondering when the annuities would arrive. It had been three years since the Great Council on Horse Creek in 1851, when the Wasichu chiefs had met with the chiefs and headmen of the local Plains tribes. Back then, the Wasichus had promised the Natives annuities, money that could be used to buy supplies from traders. But in three years, the annuities had not once arrived when promised.

High Forehead let his eyes drift across the river, where they fell on a cloud of dust thrown up by passing settlers on the rutted trail that hugged the river's southern contour. The sight of it turned his thoughts from hunger to anger because High Forehead remembered a time when the trail wasn't there, and neither were the Wasichus. It was also a time when hunger was but a strange visitor. He had heard

A wagon train headed west. Men with rifles suggest they were always prepared for a Sioux attack.

that Wasichus called it the California or Oregon Trail, but he knew it as the Holy Road.

And many traveled on it. Where they came from, High Forehead did not know, and neither did he know where they were going. Some said it was to dig in the earth for yellow metal, near the great ocean beyond the mountains. High Forehead and his friends chuckled at the rumors. Who would be crazy enough to do that?

Let them go where they want as long as they don't stay here, thought High Forehead.

But so many Wasichus came that even their passing presence caused problems. Most critically, they disrupted the northern migration of the buffalo. Not so many years ago, the shaggy beasts, the foundation of the Sioux way of life, roamed north on the plains in great herds. But the settlers' animals ate the grass that drew the buffalo north, and any buffalo that did wander into the region were scared away by their big wagons.

No, thought High Forehead, *it is not as it once was.*

In disgust, he spat in the direction of the Holy Road. Then he got up and walked back to the Brulé Sioux camp where he was visiting friends. As he approached the camp, he was surprised to see a cow. His people did not raise cattle, and he knew that they rarely raided the settlers' livestock anymore. Perhaps this one had become separated from those he had seen on the trail and had wandered towards the camp. The cow's owner could not have been too concerned about it or he would not have let it drift away. Suddenly, High Forehead remembered his hunger. He raised his rifle to his shoulder and fired. The animal fell without so much as a final bellow. Villagers ran from the camp to investigate the rifle crack.

"Oo-yee!" laughed High Forehead. "Women, gather your knives! There is a beast to prepare! We will eat well tonight."

One person, however, was not laughing. The Mormon settler who owned the cow had indeed doubled back in search of the animal. He saw the cow just as the Native raised his rifle to his shoulder, but his shout to stop him was drowned out by the rifle's crack. He watched the Natives gather quickly on the other side of the river and grew livid as he saw them butcher his cow. He marched to Fort Laramie, where he demanded to meet with the post's commander. The loosely chinked walls in the office of Second Lieutenant Hugh Flemming allowed the settler's angry voice to be heard throughout much of the fort.

"I haven't dragged that cow halfway across the continent," he bellowed, "only to have it eaten by a pack of savages! I want a new cow!

And if I can't have that, I want compensation, d…dammit. Yes, dammit!"

"Let me get this straight, sir," replied Flemming. "You're part of a Mormon emigrant train headed for Utah, and the Indians killed one of your cows."

"Those are the facts, lieutenant. Now what are you going to do about it?"

"The Indian agent is due at the fort any day. When he arrives, I'll have him look into it and assess the damages."

"It's gone beyond assessing damages, Hugh," interjected Second Lieutenant John Grattan, who was also in the office. "The Sioux are harassing settlers. They're raiding stock and pilfering supplies. The bloody nuisances beg for what they can't steal and act as if they own the place. The ink is still damp on the Horse Creek Treaty when they gave their word, their very word, that they'd let the settlers be. Well, I believe we've seen enough to know what a red man's word is worth."

"I don't know anything about this treaty and I don't give a plugged nickel for the red man's word," said the Mormon. "But I do know that I don't have time to wait for the agent. Fall's coming and I want to be settled. My partners aren't going to wait for me. I've got to keep moving."

"Hugh, I'm damned tired of the Sioux snubbing their noses at us," continued Grattan. "You give me a couple dozen good men and a fieldpiece and I'll teach them a lesson they won't soon forget. They'll run north with their tails between their legs," he assured his commander.

Flemming took a deep breath and sighed as he looked at the officer, who had only recently arrived from the East. Flemming himself was only two years out of training, but two years on the Midwestern Plains surrounded by Natives had taught him a great deal.

"Second Lieutenant Grattan, that was a view widely held at West Point, and perhaps a year at Fort Laramie hasn't been long enough to convince you otherwise. But I can assure you that it would take more than a couple of dozen men to make the Sioux turn tail. We'll wait until the Indian agent returns. That'll be all, gentlemen."

The next day Chief Conquering Bear arrived at Fort Laramie. He had heard about the dead cow and sensed that the incident might cause trouble. He just wished that it wasn't his trouble. For three years he'd shouldered the responsibility of ensuring that the Sioux remained true to the terms of the treaty that was made at Horse Creek. He often wondered how the duty came to be his. The Sioux had never had a supreme chief. But the Wasichu negotiators had insisted that there be such a person, and they had chosen him for the position. Conquering Bear knew that most of the Sioux did not recognize him as anything more than a paper chief, but he took his responsibilities seriously. Whatever he could do to prevent violence, he had done.

On this day, he came to offer compensation for the animal because he knew that if the matter wasn't dealt with, annuities would be withheld. He was escorted directly to Flemming's office, where a translator soon arrived to ensure no misunderstandings.

"Commander, I come with a pony from my own herd to offer as compensation for the cow," said Conquering Bear.

Flemming knew that the horse was more than adequate compensation, but he was no longer interested in compensation. A night of reflection and memories of West Point had convinced him that Grattan was right. The Sioux had been far too liberal in their harassment of settlers on the California/Oregon Trail, and Flemming was determined to bring them back into line.

"I'm afraid that isn't enough, chief," he replied. "I want the man who killed the cow brought to the fort so that he may face the appropriate punishment."

Conquering Bear's eyes widened and his shoulders snapped back.

"I cannot do that," he replied indignantly. "The man is not a Brulé as I am. He does not belong to my band. He is a visitor and he cannot be treated in such a manner."

"Hospitality be damned, man!" barked Flemming. "If the Sioux are going to raid settlers, you'll be held to account."

"If you want him, why don't you go up there and arrest him?" suggested Conquering Bear. "That is what you soldiers are here for."

"I'll take you up on that offer," replied Flemming. "My men will come to the Brulé camp tomorrow."

"All right," said Conquering Bear. "I'll show you his lodge. I'll show you the man."

Even as Conquering Bear rode back to his camp, he could not believe that the Wasichus would make such a fuss over a cow. But they were a strange people and he was worried. Later that night, he met in council with the headmen of his band to discuss the situation. They decided to send Old Man Afraid of His Horses to Fort Laramie the next day. Old Man Afraid was a respected leader known by the Wasichus, and they hoped he could resolve the situation.

Old Man Afraid arrived at Fort Laramie in time to see a 25-man detachment getting ready to ride out. He took particular note of the wagon gun (cannon) that they were also preparing. He was not there long when Lucien Auguste, the translator assigned to the detachment, rode up to him. Old Man Afraid could see the fear in his eyes.

"Today I go to die. I know it. You see the captain," said Auguste pointing to Grattan, who had been assigned command of the detachment. "He has been drinking, and when he drinks, he forgets that the Sioux are mighty warriors. It is not a thing to forget."

Auguste jerked the reins of his horse sharply, and the animal trotted back to Grattan. "I'm ready, but I must have something to drink before I die."

Old Man Afraid's attention turned from Auguste when he saw Flemming, who had spotted the chief and was making his way towards him.

"Is there no way that this matter of the cow might be resolved?" asked Old Man Afraid.

"Not unless the man who killed it is in irons," replied Flemming.

"You ask for too much. But so be it," said Old Man Afraid. "I am leaving."

"No, stay," directed Flemming. "If you get there and tell the news, the Indian who killed the cow will run off."

Flemming walked over to Grattan and reminded him of his orders.

"Arrest the offender. In case of refusal, determine the disposition of the Indians. Use your discretion. If you think you can take him, do so. But be careful not to hazard an engagement without certainty of success," he added.

Old Man Afraid used the distraction to slip out of the fort. It wasn't long before Grattan and his men set out on the same path. About an hour out of Fort Laramie, Grattan called his troops to a halt.

"I don't expect that we'll need to use our guns, but load them anyway," he directed. "I hope to God that we'll have a fight, and once I give the order, you may fire as much as you damned well please."

Before the troops reached Bordeaux's trading post about eight miles downstream, Grattan ordered a halt so that the cannon could be loaded. At Bordeaux's, the lieutenant sent word to Conquering Bear asking him to come to the post. While the troops waited, Auguste, fortified by booze, began riding his horse wildly near the Brulé camp, which was only a few hundred yards away.

"The soldiers will give you a new set of ears, so that you will better understand the white man's orders," he declared. "I will eat your hearts before sundown!"

"He's going to cause trouble, Lieutenant. Let me lock him up in my post," pleaded Bordeaux.

"No, I might need him." Grattan cupped his hands around his mouth and shouted, "Shut up, Auguste!"

His order had little effect on the translator, but he was soon forgotten with the arrival of Conquering Bear, who was accompanied by Old Man Afraid and other headmen. Grattan again demanded the offender, and again Conquering Bear explained that he could not turn over a man who was not a member of his band. Getting nowhere with the obstinate chief, Grattan turned to Old Man Afraid.

"Will you go and ask High Forehead to surrender?"

Anxious to defuse the situation, Old Man Afraid agreed. It wasn't long before he found High Forehead. He discovered him with some Miniconjou friends, all loading their muskets.

On hearing the request, High Forehead replied, "Last year the soldiers killed three of us. And again this year, as we sat by the road, a settler shot at us and hit a child in the head. The child still lives. Our chief, Little Brave, is dead, and we want to die also."

When Old Man Afraid relayed the message to Grattan, the officer steeled his jaw. Conquering Bear did not like the look.

"Commander, let me give more ponies for the cow," he offered. "Surely that will resolve the matter."

His blood hot, Grattan ignored the suggestion and barked to his men, "Cap your muskets. We're marching into the Brulé camp to take High Forehead."

"Lieutenant, you're going into a very bad place," said the trader Bordeaux in disbelief. "You'd better prepare yourself well."

"I've got two revolvers with 12 shots each," replied Grattan.

"Then take them out of your holsters and have your fingers on the triggers," advised Bourdeaux.

The soldiers marched the short distance to the Miniconjou lodges. Grattan ordered that the 12-pounder be trained on the dwellings and then spread his troops out in a line extending from both sides of the cannon. Grattan sent word to High Forehead, who was standing at the entrance of his lodge, to surrender.

"Tell him," High Forehead directed the messenger, "that I will not surrender. The Wasichus have treated us poorly. I am willing to die. Is he?"

Aware that the situation was becoming desperate, Conquering Bear finally asked High Forehead to give himself up. When he refused again, the chief offered Grattan a mule if he would only wait for the arrival of the Indian agent. He heard Auguste relay his message, but he was not sure he did it effectively under the influence of alcohol. Grattan wasn't inclined to listen in any case.

As they talked, the Sioux warriors began to spread out. They were joined by those from the Oglala camp upriver—hundreds of them.

Grattan caught sight of their movement, and frustrated by the stubbornness of High Forehead, shouted to his men, "Show them we mean business!"

A shot was fired. A warrior fell.

"Hold your weapons!" Conquering Bear called to the braves. He hoped that the Wasichus would pull back now that they had their blood. Another musket cracked, and Conquering Bear fell to the ground, wounded. The Sioux attacked. Within minutes, all but one of Grattan's detachment, including the translator and Grattan himself lay dead. The soldier who survived died a few days later.

Following their victory, the Sioux packed up the camps on the North Platte and headed north. But the United States government would not forget the death of Grattan and his men. By the following year, soldiers were in pursuit. The Grattan affair provided the spark that exploded into 25 years of warfare on the Midwestern Plains. It was also the event that sent a lonely, awkward boy named Curly on a path to become the greatest of Sioux warriors.

All this over a cow. And the funny thing was that the Sioux didn't even like beef—they found it too sweet.

〰〰〰

As it made its way northeast to the Running Water (Niobrara River), the Brulé camp was still abuzz with the defeat of the Wasichus. Curly and his family joined with the Brulé because it was the tribe of his father's wives, a common practice during times of unrest. As Curly rode, his eyes scanned the horizon. To the east were the Sand Hills and to the northwest, Pine Ridge. But Curly was not so interested in geography. He was watching for Wasichus. There had been much discussion among his people that the soldiers would soon follow, their rifles ready.

Curly rode with Lone Bear and his brother Little Hawk. He wished that Hump was with them, but as a warrior who had already participated in several raids Hump had duties to perform on the journey. The three separated from the main body of the traveling Sioux, as boys commonly did, and trotted along behind at some distance. Little Hawk was still absorbed in the recent fight.

"No!" he exclaimed.

"It is true," replied Lone Bear. "Curly did it as well. Ask him."

"Is it true, Curly?" asked Little Hawk. "Did you lift your breech-cloth as you stood above the body of the half-breed interpreter?"

"What Lone Bear says is true, brother. You heard the offensive words that he threw at our people. He deserved the strongest of insults in return."

"Did you see the Wasichu chief?" asked Little Hawk. "Twenty-four arrows found their mark! I counted them. He looked like a porcupine."

Curly and Lone Bear laughed. Neither doubted that Grattan had got what he deserved.

"I would like to know the warrior who sent the arrow through his skull," said Little Hawk. "His is an arm to be reckoned with."

Curly's left hand slipped to his bow arm and squeezed the still thin, immature muscles.

"Too bad we're moving north," sighed Lone Bear. "There are not so many settlers along the Running Water. No more wagons to raid."

"Yes," agreed Little Hawk.

As boys who were not yet warriors, the threesome's raiding activities had been limited mostly to shouting war whoops as they rode close to a passing wagon. Occasionally, they crept into camps at night to steal items that the settlers had left carelessly unsecured. The greatest prize of the trio had been a kettle. An acquaintance had once taken a rifle and had been the talk of the camp for days.

Curly was not so upset at moving north. He had seen enough of the Wasichus and was pleased to get away from them. It was not that he feared them, although he respected their weapons. No, Curly simply did not like them. He grew up on the stories of the buffalo herds that rolled across the prairie in a great unbroken wave. Old men laughed as they remembered a time when an unskilled hunter might grow fat, the animals were so easy to find and kill. It was that way no longer, and Curly heard the bitterness in the voices of his people as they talked of the Wasichus and their Holy Road and the long journeys to find the buffalo. Some Sioux were no longer interested in hunting the animal. Curly shuddered as he thought about them, the Laramie Loafers. How was it possible that warriors preferred to live near the fort and depend on the Wasichus' handouts rather than ride on the prairie and hunt and fight? Sometimes Curly wondered whether such people could rightly call themselves Sioux.

"Hey!" A sharp voice shouted. "You boys are too far away from the band."

Curly shot a quick glance over his shoulder. He saw a warrior with three black stripes painted on his right cheek from beneath his eye to his lower jaw.

"An *akicita*!" exclaimed Little Hawk.

The *akicita* were warriors selected to enforce band decisions. They were chosen by a small group of men who had already proven themselves as warriors or hunters. The *akicita* wielded considerable power when the camp was moving because the people's safety was their responsibility. They watched for enemies and ensured that band members remained together. Curly had seen them patrolling the fringes of the traveling camp, but this one had approached with such skill that Curly wasn't even aware of his presence until he spoke.

"Look!" mumbled Curly. "He's not just any *akicita*. His three stripes show him to be the head *akicita*."

"You boys hear as well as a Wasichu! You're too far from the band. Get back to camp," he barked.

"We'd better do as he says," said Little Hawk, who had already slapped his horse's rump to hurry its pace. Lone Bear was not far behind. Curly took a last glance at the *akicita*, wondering briefly if three black stripes might mask even the lightest of skin colors. When he came abreast of the others, far enough away from the *akicita* and close to the last of the pony drags, the boys enjoyed a nervous laugh about the episode.

To Curly's surprise, the band did not travel far that day. Rumor had it that Conquering Bear was very sick and could not be moved. Perhaps there was something to such talk because that evening Crazy Horse dashed off to the chief's lodge, with only a word that all the band healers had been summoned there. Curious, Curly followed his father.

When Curly arrived at Conquering Bear's lodge, he saw many people gathered around it. Unnoticed in the crowd, he was able to get close to the lodge's entrance. He stood and watched, hoping for an opportunity to see inside. It came as the buffalo robe that covered the entrance was thrown open.

The lodge fire was low, but it cast enough light so that Curly could see the supine form of Conquering Bear. His eyes fell on the chief's face; it was gaunt and yellowish. Curly stood there, momentarily frozen. He had seen little of death, but he sensed that Conquering Bear would soon be journeying to the Sand Hills, where the spirits of the dead lived.

Curly's anger quickly warmed him. It was not Conquering Bear's inevitable death that upset him. He knew that even important chiefs died. But few died at the treacherous hands of the Wasichus. Conquering Bear did not want to fight, yet the Wasichus attacked. It was not right! Curly ran from the lodge to the outskirts of the camp and sat on the plains looking at the moon. Soon, he heard the wails from the camp. He did not need to be told that Conquering Bear was dead.

Curly's thoughts turned to revenge. It was only with revenge that justice could be achieved. But what could he do, a boy not yet a warrior? Nothing. Curly looked out across the flat prairie, its

golden colors washed out by the pale light of the moon. He decided
that he would take the next step to becoming a man. Curly would go
on his vision quest.

Although difficult to rank the rites of passage from a boy to
a man—the buffalo hunt, the vision quest, the first raid—in order
of importance, the vision quest was of particular significance. A boy
undertook a vision quest with the hope that Wakan Tanka might
send a spirit helper to assist him on his life path. Perhaps the spirit
helper might sharpen his ability to hunt or enhance his skills on the
warpath. And while the vision quest was an intensely personal
undertaking, any assistance received in a vision was of value to the
community as well as to the individual who had the vision. Wakan
Tanka did not provide spirit helpers for personal recognition. An
individual's abilities benefited everyone.

Traditionally, careful preparations accompanied the vision quest.
After a period of fasting, a medicine man took the boy into a sweat
lodge where he was purified. His body was made strong and his
mind was cleansed of bad thoughts. The medicine man gave him
advice about performing the rituals necessary for the vision quest,
including the proper prayers, songs and attitude. Even with the
preparations, however, a young man was not guaranteed a vision,
and Wakan Tanka never blessed some Sioux. Similarly, one did not
need the preparations to enjoy a successful vision quest.

Curly, who already harbored a distaste for ritual and ceremony,
departed from camp early the next morning without telling anyone
where he was going or what he was doing. He headed east to the
Sand Hills. His horse cantered along no trail, a mountain peak in the
distance serving as his guide. Curly knew that the vision quest was
a time of humility and fasting, so he was dressed only in his breechcloth and an old buffalo robe. His hair fell loosely around his shoulders and he carried no food. The sun had not yet set when he
reached the mountain. He circled to its eastern slope, so that he
would be truly alone, and he hobbled his pony beside the lake there.
Curly climbed up the mountainside and stopped when he found

a suitable outcropping. He prayed, chanted and cried to Wakan Tanka, beseeching that he be granted a vision.

By the second night, Curly began lying on sharp rocks and placing jagged pebbles between his toes so that he might stay awake. He greeted the sun as it emerged from its lodge, but it was not a happy sight because there had still been no vision. Discouraged, Curly slipped down the mountain. When he reached his horse, he fainted. Curly later revealed to his cousin (father of Black Elk, who would become a prominent *wichasha wakan*) that he slipped "into the world where there is nothing but the spirit of all things. That is the real world behind this one, and everything we see here is something like a shadow from that world."

In this mystical world, a man appeared suddenly on horseback from the lake. He changed colors as he approached, but otherwise Curly noticed nothing striking about him. He wore plain leggings and an unadorned shirt. His face bore no paint, but the eagle feather above his long brown hair identified him as a warrior. A small brown rock was tied behind one ear. His horse traveled above the water, and when he reached the land, the animal still did not touch the ground. Although his lips did not move, Curly could hear the warrior speak.

"Never wear a war bonnet. Do not tie up your horse's tail (as was the Sioux practice), for the animal needs it to jump streams and to brush away the flies in summer. Before you go to battle, rub dirt over your hair and body."

Curly watched as the rider fought off a shadowy enemy. Arrows and bullets disappeared as they approached the man. Occasionally, his progress was impeded as his own people clutched his arms and made his riding difficult. As the man approached, Curly could see lightning appear on his cheeks and hailstones on his body. Curly continued to hear his words.

"Know that you will not be killed by a bullet or an enemy. Never take anything for yourself."

Finally, the rider could not resist the pull of his people and he stood still. A screeching hawk flew overhead, and the vision slipped away.

Curly felt a hand on his shoulder and opened his eyes. Standing above him he saw two men, but it was difficult to make out their features against the glare of the sun.

"Son, son, do you hear me?"

It was his father.

Curly's throat was dry and he could say nothing, but he nodded slightly.

"It is good to see you, brother." Curly recognized Hump's voice. "We feared that you had fallen victim to the Wasichus or the Crow."

The pair supported Curly and took him to the lake where he drank a little water. His strength somewhat recovered, Curly sat up.

"Why are you out here?" asked Crazy Horse.

"I went on my vision quest."

"A vision quest?" Crazy Horse frowned in disbelief.

He stared at his son, uncertain what to say. While he knew that a vision might come to a boy at anytime, he was also aware that such visions were usually unsolicited. To seek out a vision intentionally without performing the proper rituals was another matter. As a *wichasha wakan*, he was most upset and voiced his concern loudly and unmistakably.

"But you haven't been prepared! You didn't purify yourself or receive the words of guidance! Conquering Bear has not yet been placed on his funeral scaffold; the village is black with mourning; and yet you slipped off to go on your vision quest," he continued, his voice rising. "It is not proper!"

Curly had never seen such anger in his father, his face red and his eyes dark. Curly felt his own blood rise, and he knew that he was red with embarrassment. It was bad enough to be so openly criticized, but to have Hump hear such words was unbearable. He glanced at Hump, who was looking out over the lake. Curly's own eyes dropped to the ground.

Perhaps he had not done the right thing, but that was difficult to believe since he'd received a vision. Curly considered telling them about what he had seen but thought better of it. Hump helped him onto his horse, and Curly followed them back to camp, listening to his father's mutterings during the entire journey.

~~~~~

For days, Curly avoided others in the camp, which few saw as unusual in the solitary and quiet boy. But it was different this time. Curly was confused. He did not know what to make of his vision and was reluctant to share it with anyone. But a friend sensed his troubles. As Curly sat on the edge of a stream tossing pebbles into a still pool, Hump approached him.

"You won't catch the fish that way, brother," said Hump.

Curly chuckled and replied, "I guess not."

Hump always raised his spirits. Hump moved closer and sat next to him, wondering how best to address the private matter of the vision quest.

"You found what you sought in the Sand Hills?" asked Hump.

Curly gave a noncommittal grunt.

"It's just that you've said nothing about it," continued Hump.

"My father was in no mood to listen," replied Curly.

Hump nodded. "He was not pleased. But we both know that it was not usual for him to act as he did. He had responsibilities that weighed heavily upon him."

"It was not good for my *kola* to hear what he had to say."

"If anyone should hear such speech, it should be a *kola*," comforted Hump as he placed his arm around Curly's shoulders. "Who better to understand and share in misery?"

Curly shrugged.

"He did sound like a rutting bull buffalo," observed Hump. Curly laughed again. "I think his words should be as the snow that fell last winter, gone and forgotten."

Curly looked at Hump and smiled. Hump squeezed him with his embracing arm. Curly remained quiet and thought about whether he should tell Hump of his vision. Successful vision quests were rarely revealed, but Curly needed to share his experience. He felt that he could speak to no one other than the young warrior who sat next to him, the one who made him feel so at ease.

"I want to tell you what I saw," said Curly.

"So Wakan Tanka did bless you!" exclaimed Hump. He understood the seriousness of the situation. "I am listening."

Curly described the man on horseback floating across the lake and the shadowy figures that sought to pull him under. He spoke the words he had heard.

When he finished, Curly sighed, "Not to wear feathers or to take goods on raids. It hardly seems like a warrior's vision."

Hump remained silent as he thought about what Curly had said.

"A vision is often not as it seems. I know there is meaning here that I do not understand. Your vision needs to be explained by one who knows the language of Wakan Tanka."

Curly looked at Hump.

"What should I do?"

Hump could see the uncertainty in his friend's eyes.

"Go and see Horn Chips. He is thoughtful and wise and not so old as to have forgotten the occasional rashness of youth. Come," said Hump, standing. "I will take you to him."

Hump grasped Curly's hand and helped him to his feet. Before he let go, he placed his other hand over Curly's.

"Do not worry brother. Even one as young and ignorant as I am knows there is greatness in your vision."

The two rode back to camp in search of Horn Chips. Known also as Encouraging Bear, or more commonly, Chips, he was perhaps in his early 20s and already a medicine man. They found his lodge separate from the main body of the camp.

"Chips, are you there?" called Hump. One did not walk into the lodge of a medicine man unannounced because the lodge held secrets that were not meant to be shared.

Chips stepped out of his lodge.

"Hump and Curly. I have been waiting."

Curly looked at Hump, who shrugged.

"You know then," said Hump, "that Curly wishes to speak to you about his vision?"

Chips said nothing and reentered his lodge.

"Follow, brother," advised Hump. "I will see you later."

Curly hesitated briefly and then stepped into Chips' lodge. An unfamiliar pungent odor filled Curly's nostrils. It was dark, the small fire not enough to bring solid form to many of the shapes inside. It was just as well because Curly knew that medicine men sometimes used strange equipment, and he was more comfortable not seeing it. Chips sat to one side of the fire, leaving the place of honor across from the entrance open.

Curly was about to sit near the entrance when Chips spoke.

"Sit here." He pointed to the place of honor.

Curly's knees trembled as he sat, and then he remembered suddenly that he was supposed to give Chips an offering.

"I have come with nothing," he stammered.

"In your life you will give plenty," replied Chips. "Today your dream will be enough. Tell me of it."

Curly told him what he'd seen. All the while, Chips was gently rocking, humming a song and smoking his pipe. Curly felt the air grow stuffy and stale.

"Hmmm," muttered Chips when Curly had finished. "Perhaps you wondered why I asked you to sit in the place of honor. I know those who visit my lodge. I see lives yet to be lived, greatness before it is given expression in this life. Like the path of the moose through a thicket of dead trees and thorny bushes, your journey will be a difficult one. You will take it alone but you will benefit many."

Chips fell silent and puffed on his pipe. After some time, Curly felt that he must be finished, and he began to stand. Chips raised a hand; it held Curly still.

"Wakan Tanka has been generous with you, brother," said Chips. "Wakan Tanka has given you protection. You will be a warrior who stands apart, a solitary butte rising from the flat prairie. See me

Chips (Horn Chips) and his wife taken in 1907. Chips was
a medicine man and Crazy Horse's confidant.

again before you go on your first raid, and we will make certain that
you understand what must be done."

Curly left the lodge dumbfounded. A leader? A great warrior?
Chips had seen those things in his vision? Wakan Tanka did work
in mysterious ways.

Curly remained excited for days and was still in a good mood
when word came of a buffalo hunt. He was eager to participate and
joined the hunting party. Others learned something of his skills on

that occasion. Curly located the herd by using the tried-and-true method of placing his ear to the ground and listening for the drumming of the buffalo's pounding hooves. When the hunters found the herd, Curly killed the first buffalo. Later that evening, Hump composed and sang a song praising his young friend's efforts. A reluctant Curly would not be drawn into the celebratory circle despite Hump's pleas. Eventually, Curly slipped away from the camp, away from the crowd.

In the Moon of the Falling Leaves (November), the bands finally made their way north for the winter. They stepped lightly because their parfleches were full of *papa* (dried buffalo meat), but the journey was subdued because the memory of Conquering Bear's death weighed heavily. Brulé warriors wanted to avenge his death, but the mood of the camp was against such action at this time. Nevertheless, warriors usually did as they pleased, and four braves, including Curly's uncle Spotted Tail, slipped back down to the Holy Road and attacked a mail wagon. They killed three people and took $20,000. The Sioux had no use for the money so most of it ended up in the hands of the trader Jim Bordeaux.

Before the Moon of the Popping Trees (December), the Brulé were at their winter camp north of the Smoky Earth River (White River). The winter dragged for Curly, who found little to do. Hump was mostly preoccupied with the other warriors. Curly was not interested in playing the games of the boys because he felt that he was beyond them. He had killed buffalo and had made a successful vision quest, but he longed to demonstrate his courage. To do that he needed to raise his war club in a raid, a carefully planned strike against the enemy to steal horses or, occasionally, for revenge. The objective was rarely to kill. Much more important was taking first coup—striking an enemy with one's coup stick or other weapon before anyone else did.

Curly had gone on raids for about two years but in the role of apprentice and servant, watching most of the action from a distance. Most Sioux boys were first exposed to raids in such a manner. They were responsible for doing assigned tasks and watching what was done so that they could later put into practice what they observed. The boys were also subject to jokes and pranks. All willingly accepted the work and gibes because it meant a great deal to be invited on a raid in any capacity, and boys would endure many such raids before they were permitted to demonstrate their own skill. At the age of 14, Curly knew that his time was near, but it would not come during the winter while snow was on the ground. It was not the Sioux way to raid then.

Curly's opportunity finally came the next year, during the Moon of Making Fat (June), in 1855. The bands had gathered for a buffalo hunt north of the Platte River in early spring. Plenty of buffalo were killed, and the hunters did not need to be concerned with bringing in food for many weeks. It was just as well because after the long winter, thoughts had turned to raiding. Warriors made plans to steal horses from the Pawnee and Omaha, traditional enemies of the Sioux, and 500 raiders soon made their way south to lower Platte country.

Curly rode with them, no longer as an apprentice. As they slipped around the headwaters of the Running Water (Niobrara River), he still tingled with the excitement he had felt when his father had approached him some days earlier.

"I have counted coup. I have seen the blood of friends and enemies soak the ground. Still I have never been a great warrior," admitted Crazy Horse. "It was not my dream. But I know what greatness demands. A strong arm and a strong heart."

Curly's father fell quiet for a moment.

"Even those may not be enough," he finally continued. "Without the favor of Wakan Tanka, little is achieved. With it, little is impossible. Many things will be possible for you, my son."

These were powerful words from his father, and Curly's eyes grew wide as he listened.

"You have a fast pony and a sharp knife?"

"Yes," Curly replied.

"You will also need this."

Depiction of the Sioux hunting buffalo

Crazy Horse gave Curly a war club, a long stick with a stone attached by a rawhide thong at one end.

"Use it to take coup," instructed Crazy Horse.

Curly held the war club tightly in his hand. He liked the feel of the stout, unbending poplar shaft and the gentle pull of the fist-sized stone.

Crazy Horse placed his hand on his son's shoulder.

"Your stories will be told by warriors around the fires. Old men will shake their heads in amazement and the eyes of young boys will open wide in awe."

Curly left his father, pleased by what he heard, but uncertain about its meaning. He had not told his father of his vision, so Crazy Horse could not know that it spoke of Curly's path as a warrior. Perhaps his father had had his own dream? Curly didn't wonder about it too long. He ran to tell Hump that he would be joining the raid and then he visited Chips. The medicine man reminded him of the proper care of his pony and advised that he not take anything.

The raiding party traveled for a few days before dividing at the Loup Fork of the Platte River (in south-central Nebraska). Half the warriors went west down the Platte River in search of the Pawnee, while the others rode east in search of the Omaha. Curly joined his uncle Spotted Tail and headed east.

Scouts found a village and reported more lodges than villagers. Perhaps some were away hunting buffalo. Still, the Sioux warriors approached the village cautiously. Spotted Tail had given an order that none should attack before he gave the signal. Curly noticed the akicita, who ensured that Spotted Tail's orders were obeyed. When his uncle gave the signal, war whoops filled the air and the Sioux exploded into the village.

They caught the Omaha by surprise, and the village was quickly in chaos. Women screamed; infants cried; dogs barked. Some of the men shouted words of encouragement, but the fleeing villagers took no heed. Some carried a few hastily taken belongings, but most did not even look back as the Sioux razed their village.

Curly sat on his horse and simply watched. His stillness wasn't because of fear or shock, but of simple amazement. Sioux warriors rode tall through the camp, some firing arrows, others swinging war clubs and coup sticks. Long had he dreamed of this moment, and what he saw was everything he imagined that it would be.

Suddenly, he caught a movement out of the corner of his eye. In the nearby brush he saw a stealthy figure. Quickly, Curly notched an arrow and let it fly. The person staggered and fell. Curly jumped from his pony, slipping out his knife as he did so. He would have his first scalp, on his first raid! When he reached the fallen Omaha, he discovered it was a woman, and his heart sank. Curly stood over the body, revulsion overtaking him. He knew that killing a woman was acceptable. His people did not see it as wrong. Some even considered coup taken on women to be of special merit because they were carefully protected by warriors. Yet Curly could not help feeling that he should not have killed her. Some years later he would state that he disagreed with the Sioux practice regarding the taking of female lives. As he stood there thinking about the act, another Sioux warrior jumped in front of him and ripped her scalp free. Curly did not interfere.

Spotted Tail called an end to the attack. Ponies had been taken and the half-French chief of the village, Logan Fontenelle, had been killed. It had been a good day. Later that night, as the Sioux celebrated the victory, Curly heard a song composed for him.

> *A brave young man comes here*
> *But a foolish one*
> *Without a good knife.*

Curly knew that the words were in jest, but he reflected bitterly that it was not the song that he had heard in his dreams. He was still upset when he crawled under his blanket to sleep that night. Although he was in a mood to be alone, he was joined there by Hump, as was the usual practice of *kola*s. Curly remained quiet as Hump settled in beside him. Hump did not need to be told how the events of the day had affected his friend, and he knew that words would not ease his pain. He slipped an arm around Curly and drew him close. For a brief second Curly went rigid. Then he relaxed and allowed himself to be pulled tight. Soon he was no longer thinking about the song.

After the embarrassment of the raid on the Omaha, Curly longed for another opportunity to prove himself as a warrior. It would be many months before an occasion presented itself, when the man that the Sioux would come to know as the Hornet, Brigadier General William S. Harney, was buzzing across the Plains. Wary Natives had already learned to avoid his sting.

It had taken the War Department months to organize a response to the Grattan fiasco. While some officials believed that the arrogant young officer had shown poor judgment that summer day in 1854, even they realized that the Sioux could not go unpunished. Inaction might give Natives the impression that the army would sit idly by while its own were killed. And so William Harney, a veteran of the Mexican War, was dispatched to the Midwestern Plains. His orders were clear: teach the Sioux a lesson and don't be shy about it.

Harney was a most willing teacher. He viewed Natives as inferior to whites, a common view of the period, and when pressed for details on his mission, he declared, "By God, I'm for battle—no peace."

In mid-July 1855 he was making plans and organizing his troops at Fort Leavenworth, Kansas. A month later, he was at Fort Kearny on the Platte River, with 700 men under his command. They set out on August 24, marching along the California/Oregon Trail to Fort Laramie. At the fort, they were to head northeast and march back to Fort Pierre on the Missouri River. They were to attack any Natives found along the route.

Harney's command was not large, especially given the thousands of Sioux warriors north of the Platte River. But in the 1850s, the War Department knew relatively little about the Sioux. Those with whom the army had the most contact, the Laramie Loafers, were poor examples of Sioux character and attitude. Fortunately for Harney, the Sioux had no tradition of fighting as a unified body. And even the bravest of Sioux warriors were unprepared for Harney's bloodthirsty attacks.

The first to encounter Harney was Little Thunder's band of Brulé, camped in the Blue Water Creek valley on the North Platte River in southwestern Nebraska. Some Miniconjou, Oglala and Cheyenne were camped nearby and, in total, the Natives numbered about 250. Curly and his uncle Spotted Tail were among that number.

Little Thunder was aware that an attack was imminent. In late summer, Thomas Twiss, the Indian agent for the Upper Platte Agency, had sent messengers out to the Native bands to inform them that the army was coming and that it was intent on revenge. Hundreds of Sioux had traveled to Fort Laramie, where Twiss assured them that they would be safe. However, Little Thunder's camp had enjoyed a good buffalo hunt and needed time to prepare the meat so decided not to travel to Fort Laramie with the others. It was a fatal decision.

Harney considered all Natives who had not returned to Fort Laramie to be hostile—identified by the American government as enemies—and rumors had it that Little Thunder's band, in particular, had been harassing settlers on the California/Oregon Trail. Army scouts discovered the Brulé camp on September 2, and after a rousing, derogatory speech about the Natives, Harney advanced on the camp at dawn the following day. His troops quickly surrounded the camp. In hopes of averting violence, Little Thunder rode out to parley. He met with Harney, and they spoke through an interpreter.

"We are making buffalo. We bother no one," said Little Thunder. "My people see the Wasichus with their guns, and they fear you have come to do bad things."

"Are you not Sioux?" asked Harney.

"Brulé Sioux," said Little Thunder.

"The Sioux killed Lieutenant Grattan and his troops," barked Harney. "They attacked a mail train and stole money. They harass settlers."

"Who can control young men?" asked Little Thunder, his open hands raised. "I am friendly and do not wish to fight."

General William S. Harney (1800–89), taken in the early 1860s.
Harney enjoyed success fighting in the Mexican War before he was
recalled from a European vacation to lead a punitive expedition
against the Sioux to avenge the deaths of Lieutenant Grattan and
his command. At the Battle of Ash Hollow in September 1855,
Harney's first major offensive against the Sioux, his troops killed
close to 100 men, women and children. Eastern critics nicknamed
him "Squaw Killer" Harney for his ruthlessness, but the Sioux knew
him as "the Hornet," whose sting they wished to avoid. Sioux
delegations met with Harney throughout the fall of 1855 and the
spring of 1856. Eventually, they surrendered the warriors
responsible for violence on the Holy Road and pledged to be
peaceful. Harney's mission was deemed a great success.

The Brulé chief then held out his hand to Harney, who refused to take it. Little Thunder grew uneasy.

"You are safe until you return to your band. Tell your people that a battle is necessary to settle our differences," advised Harney. "If you do not wish to be hurt, get out of the way as quickly as possible."

Little Thunder rode back to camp. He was there only minutes before Harney gave the order to fire. The Battle of Ash Hollow was a massacre. Greater numbers and new, long-range rifles gave the army an insurmountable advantage. Desperate Sioux tried to defend their village. Warriors placed their lives in peril hoping to give women and children the opportunity to escape. Spotted Tail was one of the last to flee, and he did so only after sustaining four wounds. When the 30-minute battle ended, 86 Natives were dead, and 70 women and children were captured (including Spotted Tail's wife and daughter). The village and its possessions were under the army's control, and Harney had lost only four men.

Curly was hunting and not in the village during the attack. He heard the gunfire and the distant screams and returned quickly. As he neared, he was aware of an eerie silence that had replaced the crack of guns and unsettling screams. Closer to the village, the silence was broken by an uneven chorus of moans and groans. The cries of infants pierced the still air. Unsure what the sounds meant, Curly was worried. Everything was clear when he saw the village. Few tipis were left standing and, of those, their shredded coverings flapped in the breeze. Some Wasichus were on the outskirts of the camp, while a handful of others walked through it. Curly slipped off his horse and quietly covered the final distance to the village. Hidden in the bushes, he froze in horror at what he saw.

Amidst the broken pony drags, the overturned pots and the scattered drying racks were the bodies of his people. Many were injured, and the dead were mostly scalped. Curly's stomach turned when he saw the bloody marks that showed where the Wasichus had disrespectfully scalped dead women. As he looked at the destruction, he wondered numbly how it could have happened. A whole Sioux village destroyed.

His thoughts were interrupted when he caught sight of movement in the nearby brush. Was it a Wasichu? He dropped to the ground and slowly circled around the far side. He crept quietly through the tangle until he was close enough to see that it was a Native woman. On the ground at her side was a dead infant.

"Sister," called Curly quietly, hoping not to startle her.

Her head jerked towards the sound.

"Sister, it is all right. I am Curly," he said as he helped her to her feet. Curly could see that the Cheyenne woman was weak.

"I am Yellow Woman. This was my son. His father lies dead in the village," she explained, her quiet voice cracking.

"Where are those who are not dead?" asked Curly.

"Some are captured. Others have fled, chased by the Wasichus," she replied.

"Come," said Curly. "We will find them."

Retreating to a safe distance, Curly fashioned a pony drag and placed Yellow Woman on it. While they searched for survivors, he learned that she was a niece of Ice, a famous Cheyenne medicine man. They spent a long and quiet night together, and the next day they found a group of villagers who were alive and free.

Curly was fortunate to arrive when he did. Harney had ordered his men to pursue the fleeing Natives, so few Wasichus were in the village. When the recall was given, the soldiers were ordered to search and destroy the Sioux village. Lieutenant G.K. Warren recorded how indiscriminate the soldiers were in their attack.

...I went with others in search of the wounded. The sight on top of the hill was heart-rending, wounded women and children crying and moaning, horribly mangled by bullets....One young woman was wounded in the left shoulder, the ball going in above and coming out below her arm. I put her on my horse. Another handsome young squaw was wounded just below her left knee, the same bullet hit her

baby in the right knee....I had a litter made, and put her and the child on it. I found another girl about 12 years old lying head down in a ravine and apparently dead. Observing her breath, I had a man take her in his arms. She was shot through both feet. I found a little boy shot through the calves of his legs and through his hams. I took him in my arms.

William Harney saw all this too, yet he had a clear conscience. Soldiers found evidence implicating the band in the Grattan affair and in the raid on the mail train. That was all the justification he needed. Reports of his overwhelming victory brought praise from army superiors. President Franklin Pierce spoke of a new hero on the Midwestern Plains. Others, hearing reports like Warren's, preferred to label him a "butcher" and a "squaw killer." Indeed, in some quarters he became known as Squaw Killer Harney, but the self-righteous Harney was less interested in the praise or disdain of others than he was in ensuring the success of his mission. On September 9, he continued on to Fort Laramie. Along the way a band of Natives raided the army's livestock. Harney dispatched a troop of cavalry to bring in the culprits, but they were unsuccessful.

The general took out his frustrations on the Natives at Fort Laramie when he arrived there a week later. Natives watched with great concern and some trepidation as Harney marched the Sioux captives into the fort. Their mood did not improve when Indian agent Twiss informed them that their annuities were to be withheld. The order had come from Harney. The act was a particular blow to the Laramie Loafers, but it had a wider impact because many Natives were gathered around the fort. Most were there on Twiss' advice and few of those had been able to hunt for their winter supply of buffalo. Harney ordered Twiss to arrange a meeting of the chiefs and headmen, where he explained the new order of things.

"The Great Father gives his presents to friends. He has discovered many enemies in Platte River country. He will not give presents to his enemies," said Harney as he observed the faces of those gathered.

"Instead of presents, there will be war, which you have brought on yourselves," declared Harney. "The only conditions on which you can expect peace are the prompt delivery of the murderers of the mail party in November last, the restoration of all stolen animals and a pledge on your part to keep the road through your country open and safe for all travel.

"I will be back when the snow melts if these demands are not met," warned Harney.

Harney did not expect the Natives to remain peaceful, but he did want to give them an opportunity to change their ways. His actions and words proved effective. On the march to Fort Pierre that began on September 29, a week after the council, the army sighted no Sioux, although the territory was a traditional hunting and wintering ground for some of the bands. Just as revealing in mid-October was the surrender of three Sioux responsible for the attack on the mail coach, including Spotted Tail. Surrender was a concept foreign to the Sioux, and the courage that the act required is only understood when it is known that the trio sang their death songs as they approached the fort. They fully expected to die, and they were ready to do so for the good of their people.

In late fall, Spotted Tail and the others were transported to Fort Leavenworth, Kansas, but their fate was not immediately decided. Two boys had also participated in the raid, and their surrender was awaited. When that proved impossible—one was sick and one camped too far away—two other young warriors surrendered instead. They joined the three warriors in Fort Leavenworth in December. In mid-January 1856, they learned that President Pierce had pardoned them because he was seeking a way to minimize violence on the Plains and to silence Harney's critics.

Spotted Tail returned to his people a changed man. He had seen much in the strange, unknown country south of the Platte River. He saw large towns of Wasichus and many other settlers headed west. The Kaws, the local Natives, were confined to a reservation. They had abandoned tipis and leather dress for the houses and cloth of

Spotted Tail (1823–81), taken in the 1870s; Brulé Sioux chief and
Crazy Horse's uncle

the Wasichus. He even saw farms on their land. Were there no buffalo to hunt? Spotted Tail had seen none. With the evidence before
his eyes, the Brulé leader concluded that the Wasichus were a people to be reckoned with. They were too many to fight. The warrior
decided that the only hope for his people was peace, and he decided
that he would convince his people of that necessity.

Harney's terrifying act along the Platte River had an impact on the Sioux every bit as profound as that experienced by Spotted Tail during his southern journey. In late 1855, Harney called for a council to be held at Fort Pierre in March 1856. He was anxious to know the Sioux's reaction to his declaration of the previous fall. Messengers advised bands that those who failed to attend could expect an encounter with the Hornet's sting. The warning was enough for many Sioux leaders, and band delegations came. Some had felt the effects of a winter without white trade goods, a situation they did not wish to repeat. The Sioux agreed to leave those who traveled the Holy Road in peace, and they allowed a road to be opened between Fort Laramie and Fort Pierre. When Harney told them he had selected chiefs to act on their behalf, everyone willingly accepted the paper chiefs. The Sioux rejected nothing that Harney demanded. For his part, Harney agreed to issue annuities again.

Curly was likely at the Fort Pierre council, and he would not have been pleased with the decisions of Sioux leaders. Young warriors rarely agreed with the often-conservative words and actions of older band members, and most undoubtedly shared Curly's anger. His people behaved as if they'd been defeated, although they'd only lost one battle. The Moon of the Snowblind (March) had been a terrible month. Curly could not wait for summer and an escape to the north away from the Wasichus.

CHAPTER THREE

A Warrior Emerges

IN THE SPRING of 1857, Cheyenne warriors camped near the Smoky Hill River in northern Kansas received word that the band's medicine men Ice and Dark wanted them to gather at a small lake nearby. Many speculated about the medicine men's intent, suspecting it had something to do with the white newcomers. Recently, confrontations with soldiers had occured in central Kansas and with Rocky Mountain-bound prospectors traveling the Smoky Hill Trail through Cheyenne territory. Sioux warriors, who were wintering with the Cheyenne, had also reported that many more white men were seen north of the Platte River.

Yes, agreed most of the warriors. *Ice and Dark had a vision that might aid us in dealing with the white man.*

Like the Sioux, the Cheyenne were a Plains people, mostly nomadic and dependent on the buffalo to fulfill their needs. The Cheyenne were divided into two groups. The Northern Cheyenne occupied an area along the headwaters of the Platte River, and the Southern Cheyenne along the upper Arkansas River. In the early 1800s, the Cheyenne had been enemies of the Sioux, but by mid-century, they had become allies, banding together to fight the Crow and the Pawnee. The Cheyenne also put their mark on the 1851 Horse Creek Treaty (Fort Laramie Treaty), but they discovered, as the Sioux had, that the paper was not worth much because it failed to protect traditional Native ways and livelihoods. The Sioux-Cheyenne alliance solidified throughout the 1850s and into the 1860s, as the tribes sought to resist the great shared threat of the white man's aggressive expansion.

Curly was one of those who hurried to the lake to hear Ice and Dark. Along with Young Man Afraid of His Horses, the son of the Oglala headman Old Man Afraid of His Horses, he had spent much of the previous winter with the Cheyenne. He spent pleasant days in the company of Ice, the uncle of Yellow Woman, whom Curly had rescued at the Battle of Ash Hollow. Curly and Ice had grown close, and Ice had hinted that something important would happen this day. Curly did not want to miss it. Still, as he looked around at those gathered on the lakeshore, he felt out of place. Countless headdress feathers and scars revealed many brave warriors. Curly had participated in a raid, so he was a warrior, but he hardly considered himself battle-tested.

"Brothers!" called Ice.

Curly forgot his doubt as his eyes were drawn to the medicine man.

"We have something for you to see."

The two medicine men chanted and danced with slow and graceful movements. From his knowledge of what his father did, Curly suspected that the dance was a ritual designed to bring favor from Wakan Tanka. Curly watched as the pair crouched and submerged their hands in the water of the lake. Finally, Ice and Dark stood straight and still and looked to the warriors.

Ice held out his hand towards one of those nearest.

"Black Crow," he called. "Come forward."

The warriors fell silent as Black Crow approached the medicine men. Ice raised his hand, which brought the warrior to a stop some 25 feet from the pair.

"You have a rifle. Raise it high for all to see," instructed Ice.

Black Crow did as he was bid.

"The weapon is charged?" asked Ice.

"With powder and shot," replied the warrior.

"Then fire it!" commanded Ice.

Black Crow brought the butt of the rifle to his shoulder and pointed the muzzle out over the lake.

"You are going to shoot the waves, brother, or the breeze that causes them to roll?" asked Ice. "No. Your skill demands a worthier target. Point your rifle at me."

Uncertain, Black Crow let the rifle fall from his shoulder.

"We do not intend to join with the spirits of our ancestors this day, Black Crow. Fire your rifle at me!" commanded Ice.

The rifle cracked, and everyone saw Ice wave his open hand in front of his chest. Then he held his clenched fist at arm's length. He slowly opened his fist and black shot sprinkled from his hand onto the ground before him. Black Crow gaped in disbelief, limp arms and loose hands barely holding his rifle low.

"Load and fire again, brother," called Dark, as he presented himself as a target.

Black Crow quickly followed the instructions. When he pulled the trigger a second time, Dark caught the shot as Ice had done before him.

"We have seen this power in our dreams!" shouted Ice to the warriors. "The bullets of the white soldiers cannot hurt those who dip their hands into the water."

The warriors needed no further instructions. They scrambled for the lake, Curly among them, immersing their hands in the water. Many stood with their wet hands raised before them, watching the water run down their arms and drip from their elbows. What power this was!

In late July, the Cheyenne had an opportunity to try Ice and Dark's strong medicine. Colonel Edwin Sumner led 400 cavalry and infantry from Fort Leavenworth, Kansas, with orders from Secretary

of War Jefferson Davies, to resolve the problems caused by the
Southern Cheyenne's harassment of settlers and travelers in western
Kansas.

Davies was blunt in his direction: "No trifling of partial punishment will suffice."

Sumner discovered a large Cheyenne camp of about 300 on the
Solomon Fork of the Kansas River, some 60 miles south of Fort
Kearny, Nebraska. He planned an attack for July 29.

On that morning the soldiers assembled in their attack formation, a line three men deep. They were met with an unexpected
sight: the Cheyenne warriors had formed a bold line of their own.
It was a strategy rarely seen in Plains warfare. Most of the Cheyenne
stood openhanded before the advancing soldiers, their weapons
strapped to their sides or slung on their backs, their voices loud with
war songs. And, even more disconcerting, the soldiers could see no
trace of fear in the warriors' faces.

Why *would* they be afraid? They had the power revealed in the
dreams of their medicine men. Hands could be put to better use
catching bullets than firing weapons.

Perhaps Sumner sensed that something was up, but for a reason
never explained, he also deviated from traditional Plains warfare.
He ordered his men to draw their sabers and attack with them. The
warriors had never seen soldiers charge in such a manner, and their
unexpected tactic caught the Natives by surprise. The Cheyenne line
broke quickly. Most of the warriors ran to their ponies, where panic-
stricken women and children joined them, and they fled. Within
minutes, the Cheyenne village was deserted, and the bodies of nine
warriors and two soldiers lay on the ground. Sumner gave orders to
destroy the camp, and by day's end all that remained of the Cheyenne
camp on the Solomon Fork were the charred and smoking frames
of the 171 lodges.

Curly likely fought in the Battle of the Solomon River, but he did
not stay with the Cheyenne at their new camp. Days after the defeat,
he rode north, eager to rejoin his family. Seeing many signs of

Wasichus, he made a determined effort to avoid their trails and camps. On the long journey he enjoyed many opportunities for reflection, and his thoughts turned to the staggering violence he had witnessed over the previous few years. Curly knew about bloodshed and death; they were significant and accepted parts of Native life, especially because they were associated with such important concepts as courage, revenge and justice. But the Grattan incident, Harney's attack on the Brulé and Sumner's attack on the Cheyenne were of scales he'd never imagined.

It was not difficult for Curly to grasp that the Wasichus' involvement was the shared thread in all the incidents. Perhaps more importantly, he realized that the only Native victory came when the Sioux tribes joined to repel Grattan's attack. The Wasichu victories at the Battle of Ash Hollow and the Battle of the Solomon River came against isolated villages. He surmised that Natives needed to unite against these newcomers.

Other Natives had reached the same conclusion as Curly. Sioux leaders had decided that the Wasichus were a threat that demanded a new response. In the spring of 1857, a pipe was sent to Sioux bands. Chiefs and headmen knew the pipe's meaning: their attendance was sought at a great council. They gathered at sacred *Mato Sapa* (Bear Butte) in the summer to discuss the Wasichus. Curly arrived from Cheyenne territory when most of the tipis had been pitched. It was an incredible sight, with some 7500 Sioux camped in one great circle at the foot of the butte.

Curly found the Hunkpatila camped near the entrance to the circle, their traditional location at Sioux gatherings. His reunion with family members, whom he hadn't seen in months, was joyous. Little Hawk was especially happy to see his brother because he had important news.

"Brother, I have gone on my first raid. In truth, two, both to the west against the Crow!" exclaimed Little Hawk.

"Then you have had warriors sing your praises," teased Curly, who knew that at 12, Little Hawk had but participated as an apprentice.

"Songs, no. Jokes, yes," sighed Little Hawk.

"That will change soon, little brother," comforted Curly.

"We have heard reports of a great fight between the Wasichus and the Cheyenne," said Little Hawk. "Have you news of it?"

"I was there," replied Curly, who then described to him the Battle of the Solomon River.

"You dipped your hands in the lake?" asked Little Hawk, when he heard of what the medicine men Ice and Dark had done.

"Yes," answered Curly.

"And how did it feel?"

"It was as if some great power from the lake slipped under my fingernails and surged through my body. I felt strong. No bullet could hurt me."

Little Hawk's eyes grew large as he listened.

Curly continued the story but a familiar voice interrupted him.

"Hey-ho! So it is true. Curly has returned."

Curly looked around to see Hump. The pair embraced. After catching up on their months apart, talk turned to the great council.

"Are all the Teton here?" asked Curly.

"All but the Brulé. Apparently, Spotted Tail and Little Thunder prefer the Wasichus to their own people," replied Hump.

Curly bristled as he heard his uncle spoken of in such a manner, but he knew the truth in Hump's words.

"You have missed most of the council," continued Hump. "There was much talk. Most agreed that we were too much like the willow in bending to the demands of the Hornet. The younger warriors say that especially. Those bands from the east brought news that the Wasichus have abandoned Fort Pierre at the fork of the Bad and Missouri rivers. Perhaps the Hornet did not mean what he said."

"Many have taken courage from the northern tribes. The Hunkpapa say we should be strong and resist the Wasichus. Of course, they have seen little of the Wasichus in that country, but many heard good sense in the words of the Hunkpapa chief Four Horns. He said that the Teton Sioux should act together to resist the Wasichus, to keep them from our hunting grounds. It has been so agreed."

This was great news to Curly. He could not imagine the Wasichus defeating all Sioux warriors if they fought as one. But would they fight as one? Hump did not seem to think so.

"The agreement is mostly wind. Things remain much as they have always been," he continued. "Chiefs still control their bands with no indication that warriors will not fight as they wish."

As Curly listened to his friend, he agreed that the many strong words spoken at the council did not come with a plan for action. Curly did not think that words would be enough to defeat the Wasichus.

"Plans are being made for the Sun Dance," concluded Hump.

Although he was aware of the importance of the Sun Dance, especially because it reinvigorated the bonds of community between tribes, Curly was not much interested in the ceremony. He had never participated in the Sun Dance; he had never wanted to. Over the following week, as band members danced and sang, and warriors offered their flesh to Wakan Tanka for the good of all, Curly spent most of his time alone and away from the camp.

When the tribes dispersed in the Moon of the Black Cherries (August), they left without a plan of action to deal with the Wasichus. It was a mistake. The time was near when they would need just such a plan.

When the bands left *Mato Sapa* (Bear Butte), Crazy Horse decided that his family would travel west with Old Man Afraid's Oglala band to hunt buffalo, rather than go south with the emerging Oglala leader Red Cloud. Crazy Horse sent his family on ahead and asked Curly to ride with him. The relationship between the two had been strained since Curly's vision quest. Crazy Horse had long wondered if he had handled the situation well. He suspected that Curly had not understood his angry response, and he wanted to mend fences. Curly would soon be a warrior, and there was much Crazy Horse wanted to tell his son. Crazy Horse also wanted to listen. Was his son ready to be a warrior?

Curly suspected that the journey with his father would not be ordinary. The day before they set out, Crazy Horse had advised him to eat well because they would begin to fast with the rising sun. When they left the council grounds, Crazy Horse had a pony drag covered mostly with thick robes, which Curly knew were the makings of a sweathouse. Fasting and sweating were needed for purification. Curly thought that his father had important matters on his mind that demanded cleansing of mind, spirit and body.

Mato Sapa still dominated the northeastern horizon when they came upon a quiet creek where the water tickled the trunks of the many trees that lined its shore. Crazy Horse suggested they stop and build their sweathouse. They worked on it for the better part of the afternoon, selecting flexible willow boughs strong enough to support the heavy robes and collecting large, round rocks from the shore. When the small, dome-shaped structure was complete, Crazy Horse lit the small fire within. Curly went to the creek, filled a vessel with water and placed it near the fire. The pair then stripped down to their breechcloths. Crazy Horse took some sage from his pouch and rubbed it over his body. He did the same to his son, and they stepped inside.

The air was already hot and stuffy. Crazy Horse took the pieces of his pipe from a pouch and assembled it. He filled the bowl with *chan-sahsa* and lit it. The sweet odor of red willow bark filled the confined space. He shared the pipe with his son, and for a time, they smoked in silence with only the hissing sound of water poured on the hot rocks. Crazy Horse placed a piece of sage in his mouth, and he motioned for Curly to do the same. They chewed on it, occasionally spitting onto their arms or legs to get some relief from the heat. At first, the heat, steam, smoke, sage juice and his empty stomach made Curly feel lightheaded, but he soon felt comfortable.

"My son, your path has been a difficult one," began Crazy Horse. "I have long sensed your unease, have many times seen you slip away from ceremonies and celebrations. I did not know what to do to make things better for you. Perhaps, if I did, I would not have done them anyway. A man travels his own path, and the journey is between him and Wakan Tanka. It is not for another to interfere. Still," he added, "like the burn of a piercing arrow, your pain hurt me.

"But I have felt more than pain. I was pleased to hear your uncle say that you are a quick learner, observant and patient. I take joy in seeing your skills as a hunter. No one has ever said that Curly is greedy or selfish. And soon it will be your turn to demonstrate your courage. I do not doubt that courage runs like a deep stream in you."

"There are those who have raided with me who do not share your confidence, father," observed Curly, remembering the unfortunate episode during the raid against the Omaha.

"Ahh, yes, the Omaha," guessed his father correctly. "Who judges a warrior by his actions on one raid? Only a fool packs up his winter lodge with the first warm breeze of spring."

Even as he listened to his father say the words, Curly did not doubt his own bravery. Others saw his failure to scalp the woman as cowardice or fear, but they did not feel his heart.

It has long been the way, thought Curly. *My people see me, but they do not know me. Already I am as the warrior in my dream, pulled at by those who do not understand.*

"Father, that day in the Sand Hills, when you and Hump came to find me…," said Curly.

Crazy Horse nodded.

"I had a vision there."

Curly described what he had seen in great detail. Crazy Horse refilled his pipe and smoked as he listened.

"Who do you suppose is the warrior in my dream?" asked Curly.

"It was your dream, Curly. You are the warrior."

So it is as Chips said, thought Curly.

Crazy Horse continued to interpret what his son had seen.

"It is a powerful vision. The time is near when our people will need such a leader. That much I have seen in my dreams. There are many Wasichus. They dwell in the places the Sioux once gathered. I see no Sioux there. My dreams have taken me across the Great Plains where the grass grows long because there are no buffalo to eat it. What I see is much different from what is seen today. It is made different by the Wasichus," he observed. "It is not a good different."

The pair was silent for a moment.

"Father, I tell you today that as long as I ride as a warrior, I will fight the Wasichus and the changes they bring to our land and people," promised Curly.

Crazy Horse thought of his dream on *Mato Sapa* many years before, the dream where he saw a fearless leader of his people and thought it might be so.

He nodded.

"Let's go for a swim," said Crazy Horse as he threw open the robes that covered the entrance to the sweathouse.

Crazy Horse and Curly caught up with the others a few days later. The fall hunt was good; it filled the parfleches. The band traveled west to the Powder River, thinking little of the Wasichus because they were yet to be found there.

The summer of 1858 found Curly and his band still camped in the Powder River country. It had good, flat terrain with plenty of open space and grass to attract the buffalo. For years the Sioux and their Crow enemies had hunted in the area. Many raids had been made, and more than once, hunting parties had encountered each other and fought, but no tribe had been able to assert control over the valuable region. As the Wasichus pressed into the traditional Sioux hunting territory to the south in the Platte River country, the Sioux resolved to make the Powder River country their own.

Plenty of opportunities to prove one's courage presented themselves that summer, an ideal situation for a young man as eager as Curly. He did not hesitate when Hump asked him to join a small raiding party. Curly was pleased that his brother Little Hawk and friend Lone Bear were also invited. When they headed west in the Moon of the Black Cherries (August), Curly rode with great confidence. His father had given him a medicine bundle that held, among other sacred objects, a powder of dried eagle brain and aster flowers. Crazy Horse had advised him to sprinkle it over his tongue. In final preparation, he did as Chips had advised and threw some dirt over his pony, just as the warrior in his dream had done.

The raiding party rode west for many days, past the White Mountains (Bighorn Mountains) and the Bighorn River, until they were in a strange territory (present-day central Wyoming). Much of the land was barren. The low hills glowed white in the sun, and in the west rose the Rocky Mountains. They suspected that it was Crow territory, but the Natives they first encountered were the Shoshone who were unfamiliar to them. Shoshone scouts saw the Oglala approach, and they warned those at a nearby village. The villagers scattered onto a nearby rocky hillside before the approaching enemy warriors arrived. The Oglala made several attempts to climb the hill, but since they had little cover, they were easily repulsed.

Rather than rush into the fray, Curly held back, watching for an opportunity. He saw one as the skirmish came to a standstill. With a great whoop, he urged his pony up the slope of the hill. Recklessly, he refused to hold his head tight against his pony's neck, providing the Shoshone with a good target. However, their bullets and arrows failed to find their mark. He counted three coups before retreating to the base of the hill. He heard the Oglala shout his name, his heart thundering in rhythm with their cries, and he charged up the hillside again. He let loose an arrow at one enemy and stabbed another. Emboldened, Curly slipped from his horse to scalp his victims, but as he tore the second lock free an arrow pierced his leg. In pain, he mounted his pony and rode to safety.

Hump hurried to his *kola's* side. A quick glance at the injury showed that it was only a flesh wound and not serious.

"A good trade brother," suggested Hump. "Two scalps and the respect of all those who watched for an arrow. But look," he said pointing to the arrow, "it is a sorry piece of work. My sister could do better. I can easily remove it."

They were poor words of comfort, but they brought a weak smile to Curly's lips. Hump pushed a braid of hair from Curly's face and handed him a piece of wood.

"Bite on this as I pull it out."

With a sharp tug, Hump removed the arrow and then hurried to a nearby dead horse to cut a piece of flesh from it. He returned and strapped it on as a plaster to Curly's wound.

"Brother, I have done a terrible thing," confessed Curly.

Hump gave him his full attention.

"I saw only a brave warrior," replied Hump.

"You do not understand. I have taken scalps," said Curly as he lifted the bloody, matted locks of hair still clutched in his hand. "In my dream I was told not to take anything." He tossed the scalps away in disgust. And in all the battles yet to come, he would take only one more scalp.

Hump called an end to the raid. Coups had been counted, ponies taken and no Oglala had died. Their effort was deemed a success. When the raiding party returned to camp along the Powder River, the band held a great victory celebration. Women danced and sang and warriors described their exploits. Curly was pushed into the great circle to tell his story, and although he had every right to speak, he chose to remain silent. He was not comfortable speaking in front of his people, particularly when he spoke of himself. That night he drifted off into a restless sleep, his throbbing leg painful. He awoke the next morning his father singing just outside his tipi:

My son has been against the people of unknown tongue.
He has done a brave thing;
For this I give him a new name, the name of his father,
and of many fathers before him—
I give him a great name
I call him Crazy Horse.

Curly limped from his resting place and lifted the buffalo hide that covered the opening of his tipi. Outside, his father stood in his ceremonial robe. Behind him were the people of his village.

"Long ago, my father, Makes The Song, told me of a dream. He saw that one day my son would have the spirit of a wild horse, powerful and untamable," called Crazy Horse. "That time has come to pass. From this day I will be known as Worm. Behold the warrior Crazy Horse!"

The people looked at the young man, who was perhaps 17. In so many ways, he was different—the fine sandy hair, the pale complexion, the long, thin, straight nose. And yet, was there any doubt of his bravery or of his spirit? They sang and shouted their approval, and Curly became Crazy Horse.

In the weeks that followed, Crazy Horse worked at strengthening his injured leg. The pain subsided, but there remained a lingering stiffness. He ran often, but was usually forced to sit and rest for a time afterwards. On one such occasion, stripped to his breechcloth and relaxing in a clearing dotted with flowers and thick with the pleasant smells of summer, Woman's Dress approached him unexpectedly. Woman's Dress was from an important family, the grandson of Old Smoke and the nephew of Red Cloud. He was also a *wintke*, a homosexual. His sexuality was not a matter of much concern among the Sioux because a *wintke* dreamed his path, and others questioned neither dreams nor paths. Still, a *wintke* was different than most, and with that difference came isolation. Crazy Horse understood loneliness, and perhaps it was for that reason that he liked Woman's Dress.

Crazy Horse smiled warmly at Woman's Dress and suppressed a chuckle. Woman's Dress wore such colorful outfits. His name surely suited him. While Crazy Horse knew that few warriors would dare to wear such costumes, he suspected that many women in camp were envious of the skill Woman's Dress had with a needle.

"The warriors say you were brave when you fought the Shoshone," said Woman's Dress. "They tell of coups that would make any warrior proud."

"Some warriors enjoy telling stories," replied Crazy Horse.

"But not you," said Woman's Dress, as he sat down next to Crazy Horse. "You are so quiet, so different."

Crazy Horse shrugged. "I'd rather my arm strike than my tongue speak."

The two were silent for a moment. They listened to the birds sing and the wind whisper through the high tree branches.

"How heals the leg?" asked Woman's Dress.

"It is stiff," replied Crazy Horse.

"It must still hurt." said Woman's Dress as he let his hand fall to Crazy Horse's leg. "Perhaps if I rub it…."

Before Crazy Horse could object, a hand crept up from the scar to his thigh. Crazy Horse quickly brushed it away.

"Brother, I can deal with the pain," said Crazy Horse as he stood.

"Yes, with Hump's help," snarled Woman's Dress.

"What I do with Hump is not your concern, Woman's Dress," said Crazy Horse as he turned to leave.

Rebuffed, Woman's Dress watched Crazy Horse slip into the trees, his eyes becoming dark and vengeful. Crazy Horse hurried back to the camp, the stiffness and pain in his leg forgotten.

≈≋≈

In the early summer of 1861, two elderly Oglala men, their battles long since waged, sat near a small fire they had kindled beside a stream. Around them grew tall cottonwood trees that gave relief from the hot sun, high in the clear blue sky. The air was still, and the smoke from the fire and their pipes drifted above them like tight rawhide ropes. They were discussing a young warrior whose exploits had become the talk of the village.

"The war party against the Shoshone attracted many warriors," said Bear Claw.

"Who wouldn't want to fight Washakie?" noted Man With Club. Washakie was a prominent Shoshone chief, and he had been for many years.

Woman's Dress, taken in 1914 (with Captain Jim Cook). Known in his youth as Pretty One, Woman's Dress was homosexual, a *wintke*. His sexuality was not a matter of much concern among the Sioux because a *wintke* dreamed his path, and neither dreams nor paths were questioned. Crazy Horse and Woman's Dress were friends from childhood, but their relationship soured perhaps when a teenage Crazy Horse rebuffed overtures from Woman's Dress. Woman's Dress seethed at the rejection and swore revenge. Years later, when Crazy Horse surrendered, Woman's Dress was an army scout at Fort Robinson and conspired against his old enemy. Woman's Dress' lies turned General Crook against Crazy Horse and helped set into motion a series of events that resulted in the Oglala chief's death.

"Some were Cheyenne," added Bear Claw. "When an Oglala runner arrived at their camp to bring news of the war party, many were eager to participate. Crazy Horse was living at the Cheyenne camp, and that's how he came to know of the war party."

"The Shoshone camp was asleep when the warriors attacked," continued Bear Claw.

"It is not an easy thing to keep the young warriors quiet to allow for surprise. The *akicita* did their job well," observed Man With Club.

"Yes, and the raid was successful. The warriors took 400 ponies before the Shoshone could organize."

"Many ponies."

"Too many," replied Bear Claw. "The animals hindered the warriors' escape. The Bighorn River was still in the distance when they realized that they could not outrun the Shoshone. Seven warriors slipped back to slow the enemy.

"Crazy Horse was one of them. He hid behind rocks and trees and fired arrows at the approaching Shoshone. But there were so many that he could not remain in one place too long. He'd jump on his pony, retreat a short distance and then fire some more arrows. More than once, he charged eager Shoshone warriors who had ridden ahead of their brothers, forcing them to withdraw."

"Ungh," grunted Man With Club. He was aware of the courage demanded for such action.

"Finally, the Shoshone tired of the game. Washakie pushed the warriors hard until they were within an arrow's flight of Crazy Horse. Two warriors rode forward towards him and his brother Little Hawk, who had joined him. These Shoshone were smart," said Bear Claw. "They shot Crazy Horse's pony, then his brother's. Then two warriors charged the brothers to engage them in single combat.

"Crazy Horse called to his brother, 'Take care of yourself. I'll do the fancy stunt.'"

"How do you know his words?" asked Man With Club.

"Big Elk told me," replied Bear Claw. "He heard it from Short Bull, who was one of the warriors who rode with Crazy Horse."

"Crazy Horse waited until one Shoshone was close. He made no move, and perhaps the Shoshone thought he would have a scalp without much trouble," chuckled Bear Claw. "Then Crazy Horse bolted to one side, spun around and attacked from the other side! He pulled the Shoshone to the ground before he could lift his war club, and Crazy Horse had his scalp before the thud of his fall had faded away. The other warrior escaped with Little Hawk's arrow in his shoulder. The brothers rode away on the Shoshone's pony."

Man With Club whistled through his teeth. "There is a man! What of the other Shoshone?" he asked.

"Washakie was angry, and they chased the Oglala hard. When the Shoshone finally caught up with them, the seven warriors had rejoined the war party. The warriors were able to choose a defensible position in a thick stand of trees, and they easily met Shoshone charges. They escaped during the night and returned to their village. They carried with them the bodies of three Oglala and one Cheyenne. Following the mourning, the village held a great celebration," added Bear Claw.

"Yes," nodded Man With Club. "The songs are not difficult to imagine, especially those sung for Crazy Horse."

"Crazy Horse would have had to imagine them," replied Bear Claw. "He was not there to listen. He doesn't like to celebrate. He didn't keep the scalp, either. It was in Little Hawk's hands before the pair had rejoined the warriors."

"A brave man, but a strange one," said Man With Club.

Bear Claw grunted in agreement as he refilled the bowl of his pipe.

In the late 1850s and early 1860s Crazy Horse's name was on the lips of all Sioux who spoke of courage in battle. While there are few detailed records of Crazy Horse's activities as a young warrior, it seems that his people first took notice of his battle skills following a fight against the Pawnee in 1859. When Oglala scouts reported that the Pawnee warriors were near, Crazy Horse surged ahead of his companions in an effort to take first coup. The others were impressed. That night, following the battle, Crazy Horse sat among the bravest of the young men, and his exploits dominated the discussion.

Older warriors may have wondered whether Crazy Horse's actions were more youthful rashness than courage. But after they witnessed him in another battle against the Shoshone they wondered no more. As he charged the Shoshone warriors, Crazy Horse's pony was shot out from under him. Rather than retreat or scramble to safety, he sprang forward at the approaching enemy. In short order, the Shoshone lay dead, and Crazy Horse was riding away on the enemy's pony, shouting war whoops for all to hear.

Thunder Tail, a warrior who often rode with Crazy Horse, described an extended fight against the Crow that occurred in the late 1850s. Oglala warriors found a Crow village and attacked. "Crazy Horse rode near. But though there was much shooting he went fearlessly and rode in at really close quarters. It turned out his horse was killed, yet on foot without fear he fought, killed and left the place. There was much shooting, but he was not wounded."

The Oglala left with a small herd of ponies, and the Crow were soon in pursuit. "We withstood 10 of them who took refuge on a hill," said Thunder Tail. "Then again, Crazy Horse and Bear Stops together attacked them. They went up close, which helped. Crazy Horse first put himself in their midst and began swinging his club. So, he sifted out the Crow and they sent him on his way, trying to kill him."

The Crow failed in their effort, but they weren't about to give up. Later that summer, the Crow attacked the Oglala warriors' camp. At one point in the battle, Crazy Horse's two brothers (a mistake in Thunder Tail's account because Crazy Horse had only one brother) were under immediate threat from the Crow.

"Crazy Horse came forward and really gave them a chase, helping the two younger brothers, and they put the enemy to flight. One of the Crow he shot, seized, killed…. The Crow then cried badly and fled. From then on Crazy Horse's name was very much talked about," noted Thunder Tail. "They were encamped on the Rosebud

River when they got home. The people were very happy, and Crazy Horse was very popular."

Crazy Horse developed a unique fighting style. His friend He Dog, who rode at his side in many battles, marveled, "In critical moments of the fight, Crazy Horse would jump off his horse to fire. He is the only Indian I ever knew who did that often."

While Crazy Horse was undoubtedly a fine horseman, he didn't seem to be comfortable fighting while mounted. He did have his pony shot out from under him eight times in battle. He may also have heard that the Crow, who considered Crazy Horse the most fearless Sioux they had ever fought, had traveled to Nez Perce territory in western Idaho in search of a medicine to bring death to his ponies. Crazy Horse might have concluded that it was safer to attack on foot.

And safety was important to him. Perhaps in his youth Crazy Horse had fought impulsively, but young warriors eager to prove their courage were not usually cautious. Crazy Horse had suffered injuries as a result. Since then, however, he had more closely followed his vision and wore an amulet given to him by Chips for protection. Chips' gift was good medicine—Crazy Horse had not been injured since he began wearing it. And as he matured, Crazy Horse became more reflective in battle. He devoted a great deal of time to considering his attack and did not fight until he had a good plan and the confidence that he would win.

He Dog said, "He wanted to be sure that he hit what he aimed at. That is the kind of fighter he was. He didn't like to start a battle unless he had it all planned out in his head and knew he was going to win. He always used judgment and played safe."

One summer, perhaps in 1862, Crazy Horse was one of many Sioux who gathered on the Little Bighorn River for the annual Sun Dance. Not interested in participating, Crazy Horse spread the word that he wanted to raid and steal ponies. He had no difficulty attracting warriors to ride with him. It was well known that his raids were successful, but more than that, Crazy Horse was generous in battle.

His cousin Eagle Elk explained, "He does not attack enemy and strike coup as many times as he can. He does not count many coups. He is in front and attack enemy. If he shoot down an enemy he does not count coup. He drop behind and let others count three of the four coup counts. He takes the last coup. I do not understand why he did that. He had such a reputation that he did not have to get more of that."

Once the nearly 40 warriors had gathered, Crazy Horse addressed them. "We will head for Missouri River country. Some Brulé have told me that a war party of Arapaho, Crow, Flathead and Nez Perce is riding there. Make sure that your knives are sharp," he laughed.

In a few days they reached the Missouri River, which they could not ford on horseback. Fortunately, they encountered a herd of buffalo. They killed as many as they needed to build bull boats. The bull boat served the limited navigational needs of the Plains Natives, allowing them to easily ford streams or to travel short distances. The only materials required to build the vessel were willow boughs and buffalo hides. The pliable willow boughs were shaped into a circle six feet in diameter and entwined underneath in the shape of a basket about a foot and a half deep. Stretched over the frame was a single green buffalo hide, attached at the top with pieces of skin. As the craft dried, the skin was pulled tight to the frame. The bull boater sat in the front of the craft, and using a paddle, was swept along with the current with his horse swimming behind.

With the river behind them and their bull boats pulled ashore to dry, Crazy Horse led the warriors to a nearby butte where they planned to set a trap. He sent out two scouts to determine the location and number of the enemy. They returned quickly.

"Forget the trap," they advised. "The enemy warriors are gathering to make camp. If we wait until they all arrive, they will be too many to fight. Best to strike while they are still separated into small parties."

"Yes," agreed Crazy Horse. "Prepare yourselves to attack."

He Dog (1830–1931), taken in 1900. Crazy Horse's close friend fought by his side in many battles.

Crazy Horse made his personal preparations following closely the directions from his vision. He painted his face with a zigzag, stretching from his forehead along his nose to the base of his chin and dabbed a few white spots on his face. Crazy Horse was certain that the designs that he had seen in his vision protected him in battle. He took a handful of dirt from the ground and rubbed it between the ears and on the hips of his pony. He took more dirt, stepped in front of the pony and threw it towards the pony's tail. He repeated this from behind the pony, throwing the dirt towards the pony's head. Then he walked around the animal, brushing the dirt off. Finally, he took some dirt and rubbed it on his hands and over his head.

In their own preparations, some warriors prayed to Wakan Tanka or performed rituals revealed to them by their spirit helpers. Soon all were ready, and they set out for the enemy camp. Crazy Horse took the lead. Those behind him could see his sandy hair braided in two rows on either side of his head. Between them was an inverted spotted feather taken from the middle of an eagle's tail. Under his left arm, suspended by a rawhide thong slung over his shoulder, hung the pierced white stone given to him by Chips. He wore a shirt, breechcloth and moccasins. In his hand he clutched a Springfield rifle that he called an "open and shoot." The Crow thought it was a magic rifle that never missed its target. Many warriors would have nodded in agreement.

The Oglala made a quick strike against the enemy camp, catching the Arapaho and their allies by surprise. They took no coups but made off with 100 ponies and wasted no time in heading back to Sioux territory. After a few days' travel and no sign of the enemy, they thought they were safe and stopped to rest at a river. But the enemy warriors had not given up; they were merely waiting for an opportunity. They chose well. Before the Sioux could organize a response, half their stolen pony herd was taken. The Sioux warriors scattered on foot, some seeking safety, others trying to round up ponies.

Crazy Horse called to them, "Be brave! Fight even if we all get killed. Fight them!"

Then he turned and charged the enemy, allowing the others to get to safety. Not everyone ran, however. Half a dozen warriors joined him.

"Be of courage! Fight them!" shouted Crazy Horse. "It would not do to see the enemy kill all of us. Fight them until some get away alive. Someone must be left to tell the tale."

The barrel of Crazy Horse's rifle was hot as he fired round after round at the enemy. But he was worried. The half dozen Sioux warriors were easy targets on the stretch of grassland.

"Head for the trees," he shouted. "Up the slope, where we have herded the stolen ponies."

Carefully, the warriors slipped back into the stand of trees.

"Low Dog and Charging Cat are missing," shouted Eagle Elk.

"I'll keep the enemy busy," replied Crazy Horse. "Find them!"

Crazy Horse and two warriors stepped from the trees. "Hoka hey," they called as the two ran away from the others and drew Arapaho fire.

Kicking Bear, the only Sioux with his own pony, called a signal for the missing men to show themselves. He saw them at the base of the hill. He charged towards them, scooped them up on his pony and raced for the safety of the trees. Crazy Horse circled the trees and joined them.

"The others have gathered with the ponies," he revealed.

The enemy gave up their attack once the Sioux were in the trees. They had retrieved many stolen ponies and had achieved a measure of revenge. When they saw the enemy warriors leave, Crazy Horse gave the order to move out. They rode without rest because Crazy Horse was not certain that the enemy warriors had withdrawn. He searched for a defensible position and found a deep canyon with a stream banked by trees. He called a halt.

"We stop here. You all take a good sleep. If the enemy comes again we are not running away. But we will go into this place and stay and fight them. You must all go into this place and sleep," he advised. "Remember, if they surprise us again, we are not going to run, but we go into this place and fight them."

The enemy warriors never did show up. Soon the Sioux were at the Missouri River, which they again forded in their bull boats. A few days later, they were back at the Sioux camp on the Little Bighorn River. No one celebrated much, however. While they had taken many ponies, they had no scalps or stories of coups. Some of the

warriors were determined to redeem themselves so they planned
a raid on the Crow. When Yellow Horse, a medicine man, warned
them that he had a vision in which several warriors died, Crazy
Horse decided not to participate. It was a good decision. Two of the
warriors Yellow Horse saw killed in his dream never returned.

~~~~~

Crazy Horse did not spend all of his time fighting during the
years after he became a warrior. Perhaps he fought more than most
because he was eager to make his reputation, but even then, warfare and raiding occupied only a little of his time. Hunting dominated a man's activities, and when the parfleches were full, the men
could spend long days in leisure. The Sioux had several societies that
a man could join. Most of them were long-standing organizations,
and membership depended on age as well as ability. Given his popularity and success, several societies wanted Crazy Horse as a member, but he did not enjoy the social aspect of the organizations. He
was a member of the Kangi Yuha, the Crow Owners' Society, from
which the *akicita* were drawn. He fulfilled his obligations as an
akicita, and he became a respected lance bearer of the society
because of his fighting ability. But he had no interest in joining the
other members in their private gatherings, where they smoked pipes
and told stories.

The young men's stories were dominated by discussions of
coups and young women. Perhaps the subjects gave Crazy Horse
reason enough to avoid the social gatherings. When warriors spoke
of bravery, Crazy Horse's name inevitably came up, and he did not
enjoy being the center of attention. He was also uncomfortable
talking about young women, especially when the conversation was
of a sexual nature. Usually the braves' talk was simply bragging
about successful efforts to take the virginity of Sioux maidens, or
ribbing about failed undertakings. Crazy Horse was not inclined
to make the effort and was not interested in listening to others
detail their exploits.

A young Sioux warrior might well be confused when it came to the opposite sex. The Sioux demanded chastity of their young women. A virgin bride was important to the family because her virginity spoke of their values and, as such, it was a matter of honor and prestige. It also ensured that a suitor would give many ponies for her hand. Practice and custom were designed to ensure chastity. From an early age, boys and girls were separated in all activities, and they rarely socialized together. When girls reached their teenage years, they were chaperoned by older women. If courted, they were permitted to join their suitor under a robe, which offered a small measure of privacy. At night, they wore chastity belts or had their legs tied together. The practices designed to keep young women chaste were necessary because of the time-honored tradition of young warriors seeking to sleep with young women. Ironically, it was also the case that the practices aroused the enthusiasm of the young warriors. It was not easy to bed a young woman, and his peers respected one who managed it.

Crazy Horse never seems to have played this game, and the reasons for that can only be speculated. Shy as he was, he may not have been at ease around women his own age. He also held the memory of his mother in such high regard that he may have considered a relationship outside of marriage to be a slight to her. Although Crazy Horse was a loner, he did share a close bond with a small circle of friends, who may have provided all the intimacy he needed. The Sioux thought that sexual relations with a woman before going on the warpath weakened a man. Self-control allowed a warrior to direct his energy to fighting the enemy. Given that Crazy Horse strove to be the greatest of warriors, that one belief may have been sufficient to have him abstain from liaisons with women.

However, in spring 1862, Crazy Horse's world was rocked when he fell in love with Black Buffalo Woman, a Bad Face Oglala whom he had known since childhood. Had Crazy Horse fallen in love with anyone else, he could have expected a quick marriage because his reputation made him much sought after. Black Buffalo Woman, however, was in demand herself. Not only was she beautiful, she was also a niece of the respected Oglala warrior and leader Red Cloud. Many young warriors longed to be linked with Red Cloud through marriage.

Crazy Horse was confused by these new feelings, and he sought Hump's advice.

"Black Buffalo Woman!" exclaimed Hump after Crazy Horse had explained his dilemma. "My *kola* has a good eye, indeed."

"Yes," replied Crazy Horse, "and it sees the long line of braves who wait outside her lodge each day."

"Of course. A man does not settle for grizzled flank when the fatty hump is available," he laughed. "Do you know a warrior who would take coup on a brave when the chief is waiting to be struck?"

"I wish it *was* a battle," confessed Crazy Horse. "Then I would know what to do."

"Of that I have no doubt," agreed Hump as he put his hand on Crazy Horse's back. He saw the despair in his friend's face.

"The challenge faced by one who wishes to marry Black Buffalo Woman is to convince her family that he is a worthy suitor," advised Hump. "Her family will decide whom she marries, and you know they will want more than a great warrior as a son-in-law. They will demand many ponies for her hand."

"I have no ponies except those I ride in battle," moaned Crazy Horse. He had taken many horses in raids, but, unlike other young men who sought to build up impressive herds, Crazy Horse always gave his away. He was not interested in the trappings of wealth and was generous to a fault.

"I have a small herd; what is mine is yours," said Hump.

Crazy Horse smiled at his friend.

"But I think even those would not be enough to win her hand," added Hump.

"Then what am I to do?" agonized Crazy Horse as he shook his open hands in front of his chest.

"I think that she will not marry quickly, brother. Young women enjoy the attention of many suitors. There is still an opportunity to build up a herd," suggested Hump.

"Yes!" agreed Crazy Horse. The thought of raiding eased his troubled mind.

"In the meantime, join the line outside her tent. Take a large buffalo robe," joked Hump. "And remember that a woman likes to hear sweet words rather than war whoops, whatever your preference!"

Crazy Horse gave a feeble smile as he left his friend.

The next afternoon he prepared to meet with Black Buffalo Woman. He dressed in his best shirt and leggings. He considered painting his face, as was common during courting, but decided against it. Crazy Horse could think of nothing to paint except the designs he wore in battle, and he feared he might weaken their medicine by using them for another purpose. He selected a robe and walked to her lodge. He took long, purposeful steps that he hoped would suggest a confidence he didn't really feel. When he approached her lodge and saw the line of suitors six or eight deep, all with buffalo robes draped over an arm, his gait became less cocky. He shuffled to the end of the line.

He was not last in line for long. Others joined, and when Black Buffalo Woman finally slipped from her tipi, Crazy Horse suspected that it would take most of the night for her to talk with each of them. But as Crazy Horse set eyes on her, he knew it was worth the wait.

Black Buffalo Woman was stunning. Her long black hair shimmered as it caught rays from the setting sun. A tanned dress not much lighter than her own perfect skin and decorated with ornate beadwork hugged her body. Her lips were red and her eyes were dark, although they were difficult to see because she took care not to look at the faces of the young men. Such forward behavior would have been a sign that she accepted one man's advances. Tonight she would sit under the robe with all of them.

Crazy Horse waited for his turn. He thought he knew something about patience, but he found it difficult to keep still. This was not like

hiding in the bush waiting for an animal to kill or scouting over vast
terrain for an enemy. Those in the line talked little, a few uneasy words
about the unusually dry weather, some jokes and awkward smiles. The
line moved slowly, not at all in rhythm with the quick beating of
Crazy Horse's heart. He wondered what he was doing there.

Suddenly, he was next in line, and Crazy Horse no longer wondered what he was doing there. His legs turned into springy willow
as he approached Black Buffalo Woman. Fleetingly, he thought that
a warrior struck in the head with a war club might feel just as dazed.

"Crazy Horse, great warrior!" sang Black Buffalo Woman as she
patted the ground beside her. He sat down and pulled his legs in
tight. He looked to Black Buffalo Woman's aunt, who sat across
from them, as he wrapped the robe about them. He was greeted
with a most forbidding stare, bringing him momentary panic.

"I thought you had come to look at me," pouted Black Buffalo
Woman.

"Yes, yes," blurted Crazy Horse, as he tore his eyes from the aunt.
"Of course."

"Good," she purred. "Pull the robe over our heads."

This was not at all expected.

"But your aunt?"

"Was once a courted young woman."

Crazy Horse did as bid and soon found himself overcome by her
sweet smell. He was glad to be seated for he was certain he would
collapse if standing.

"You have not come to my tipi before," chastised Black Buffalo
Woman. "But we will forget the past. It is good to see you now."

"You are not the girl I remember playing with in the tipi when
we were young," said Crazy Horse.

"I should hope not!"

"Perhaps you are ready to stop playing?" suggested Crazy Horse,
wondering as he said it how he managed to speak such words.

"So direct!" she laughed. "I have heard that the great Crazy Horse
is a warrior of few words."

Crazy Horse felt his face flush, and he thanked Wakan Tanka that she could not see him blush under the robe.

"But I want to hear you speak. Perhaps you have a story to tell?"

Crazy Horse thought for a moment.

"There is the time I fought Washakie and the Omaha. Or perhaps my first coup against the Shoshone?"

"I don't want to hear about fighting. That talk is for around campfires, not the talk under the robe. Perhaps you have composed for me a song? You may sing it."

A song! Was he supposed to compose a song? Why hadn't Hump warned him? He thought hard, but only warriors' songs came to mind. Black Buffalo Woman began to hum gently. She wanted a song.

Crazy Horse cleared his throat and began.

The bird that flies has pretty wings,
blue or black or yellow.
The bird that flies has pretty wings,
Its feathers glimmer in the sun's light.
The bird that flies has pretty wings,
they keep it free in the great blue sky above.

Even as he sang, Crazy Horse wondered where the words had come from.

"A...pretty song," said Black Buffalo Woman, as she pulled the robe down.

"That's it?" he asked.

"There are others waiting, Crazy Horse. I have to think of them as well."

Crazy Horse stood and folded his robe over his arm. Disappointment flooded through him. It had not been at all what he expected. He turned to walk away.

"You may come and see me again if you wish," called Black Buffalo Woman.

One of a series of drawings by Amos Bad Heart Bull (1869–1913),
Crazy Horse's cousin, depicting "Sioux Early Social Life and Its
Reorganization." Entitled "Customs of the Past," this drawing
illustrates a courting scene. The couple is granted some privacy
by the robe and umbrella (a modification of traditional practice),
while other suitors await their turn to court the woman. Between
1891 and 1913, Bad Heart Bull, a scout in the United States Army,
drew more than 400 pictures illustrating the history of his Oglala
tribe using the Sioux tradition of depicting important events in
pictographs. But his work was richer in detail and content than
most previous picture writing. In accordance with tribal custom,
Bad Heart Bull's original drawings were buried with his sister
when she died in 1947.

Crazy Horse smiled, looked back and nodded. His feet seemed to barely touch the ground as he returned to his lodge.

Crazy Horse returned to Black Buffalo Woman's lodge many times over the following weeks. Other warriors were always there, but the one he saw most regularly was No Water, a prominent warrior in his own right. That and his large herd of ponies was evidence enough that No Water was his main competition for Black Buffalo Woman's hand. It was no matter; Crazy Horse did not mind competing.

About a month later, Red Cloud announced that he was going to lead a raid against the Crow. He asked both Crazy Horse and No Water to help him. Crazy Horse guessed that their performance on the raid might determine who would marry Black Buffalo Woman. He prepared carefully, and when he explained to his brother Little Hawk and to Hump the importance of the raid, they agreed to join him and offer whatever support they could. They set off in the Moon When the Cherries are Ripe (July). Crazy Horse was brimming with confidence. He might be unsure under the robe, but he knew what to do on a raid.

Matters took a strange turn a day out of the Oglala camp. No Water suddenly developed a painful toothache. He spoke to Red Cloud and advised him that the pain was too great for him to continue. Red Cloud agreed that he should return, a decision the other warriors supported. No Water's medicine was the teeth of the grizzly, and all knew it was a bad omen that his tooth should be hurting. He could do no good on the raid.

The raiding party returned two weeks later, having enjoyed great success. They had stolen ponies, taken coups and killed one Crow. Crazy Horse had demonstrated his courage and felt sure that Red Cloud would not object to his marrying Black Buffalo Woman. He was so happy that even the appearance of Woman's Dress, a day out of the village, did not dampen his spirits.

"Woman's Dress! You are not one usually seen among the warriors," said Crazy Horse.

"Yes," agreed Woman's Dress. "What I do with the warriors is not usually seen. But I have news from the village, news that is cause for celebration. For some, at least," he added.

"Tell us, then," said Hump.

"Black Buffalo Woman has given No Water a pair of moccasins. He has put them on," smiled Woman's Dress as he looked at Crazy Horse. It was the rite of marriage among the Sioux. The pair was betrothed.

Crazy Horse was crushed. Red Cloud had betrayed him! His light skin became even paler as the blood drained from his face. He kicked his pony in the midsection with a sudden jab and the animal broke towards camp.

"Crazy Horse!" called Hump, "Wait!"

"You should be pleased, Hump," suggested Woman's Dress. "Now he has more time for you."

Hump raised his hand to strike Woman's Dress, but the *wintke* bolted, laughing as he rode away.

Crazy Horse returned to his stepmother's lodge, where he stayed for a few days. He didn't venture outside, and no one dared to visit him. One morning he stepped from the lodge, the protruding quill of a spotted eagle feather visible above a face painted with a lightning bolt. With meaningful steps he strode to his pony, rifle in one hand, war club in the other. His bow and a quiver of arrows were strung around his back and a small white stone hung from his shoulder. He leaped on the animal and rode from camp, headed for Crow territory. When he returned some days later, he had a scalp tied to his side. It was the last scalp he would take, and he threw it to the first dog he saw. Then he built a sweat lodge and sat inside until he felt whole again in body and spirit.

CHAPTER FOUR

A Warrior and a Man

CRAZY HORSE HAD little contact with the Wasichus in the late 1850s and early 1860s. He stayed in the Powder River country and raided traditional Native enemies. There the game was plentiful and Wasichus were rare. To the east and the south, however, Natives were not so fortunate because white men arrived in increasing numbers during these years. Some wanted to farm and some to mine for gold while others wanted to travel the well-known trails that cut through Native territory on their journeys westward. Tribes like the Santee Sioux, the Cheyenne and the Arapaho were faced with dealing with the new, unwelcome presence. Usually, the result was war.

The Santee were an eastern division of the Sioux, and their homeland was in the territory that became Minnesota. Although they hunted buffalo, the Santee were a less nomadic people than were their western Teton relatives. They stayed closer to the Minnesota River, and because they lived more to the east, they felt the pressures of white encroachment before the Plains Natives. Change came quickly. In 1849, Minnesota became a territory, and two years later the Santee signed the Treaty of Mendota with American negotiators led by Alexander Ramsay. They ceded great parts of

Minnesota and Iowa for just over $1.4 million, which was to be paid over 50 years in both goods and annuities. The Santee also agreed to confine themselves to a narrow strip of land above the Minnesota River.

The agreement did not sit well with all of the Santee. The ongoing failure of annuities to arrive when promised and the never-ending stream of white settlers who threatened the Natives' hunting livelihood fueled their anger. In 1857, Chief Inkpaduta led his band in a devastating attack on Spirit Lake, Iowa (close to the Minnesota border), killing more than 40 settlers. Soldiers and Sioux friendly with the American government pursued Inkpaduta and his followers, but because most of the local troops were preoccupied with the Mormon War in the southwest, they had little to fear.

Inkpaduta's uprising was not enough to deter settlers, who continued to be attracted by the large tracts of open land. They arrived in such great numbers that by 1858 Minnesota had achieved statehood. Soon, homesteads bordered the Santee reservation, and state officials cast greedy eyes on the open stretches of Santee lands. They began to pressure the federal government for access, and in 1862, President Abraham Lincoln signed the Homestead Act. It authorized a homestead grant of 160 acres of public land to settlers who lived on the land and improved it for five years. Thousands packed up and headed for Minnesota, and the pressure to open reservation land increased. Relations between the Santee and the settlers soured accordingly. The most violent episode occurred in the spring of 1862, when four Santee killed three men, a woman and a girl during a target competition. Emotions on both sides ran high, needing only a spark to set the whole thing off. It came later that summer in the words of an oafish trader.

The annuities were late in arriving again. The winter had been harsh, its bite seeming sharper with each passing year. Little Crow, chief of one of the Santee Sioux bands and a signatory of the Treaty of Mendota, had heard that some traders were giving away goods on the promise that annuities would be handed over to them upon arrival. Little Crow and some of his braves visited a local trader, who proved neither sympathetic nor cooperative.

"What in hell do I care if'n winter's been tough on ya? Screw what other traders is doin'," he barked. "Only tradin' I do is when I see cash on the barrelhead. I ain't in business fer my health."

"Our people won't make it much longer," replied Little Crow. "Already the hungry children cry themselves to sleep. The weakest have died. Others will soon see their ancestors. I am begging you."

"Beg all ya want. I'm not in it fer yer health either. If yer hungry, eat grass. There's plenty o' that," he muttered as he pointed to the ground. "You folks is nuttin' but a problem. Killin' and beggin'. Soon enough, though, I won't have to deal with the likes of you anymore. A railroad's being built that's gonna come right through here. If ya think there's lotsa whites now, well, ya ain't seen nuttin' yet. Get yer red hides outta here, and don't come back less'n ya got some money."

Little Crow was against war with the whites. Since making treaty in 1851, he had adopted their ways, going so far as to build a frame house and live as a farmer. Despite mounting pressures from his young braves, he counseled against violence. But even he found it difficult to accept what the trader had said. The potent mixture of years of suffering, discrimination and racial epithets, and the news that the white man would be increasing in number turned Native frustration to anger. Little Crow would have to act before those whites arrived. He knew there was opportunity. The northern forts were empty; the Wasichus had gone south to fight amongst themselves. In August 1862, the Santee Sioux began to fight back.

Their first target was the agency that employed the offensive trader. The Santee killed him and filled his mouth with hay, a reminder to others that the Santee were to be treated with greater respect. The warriors then rolled down the valley of the Minnesota River, destroying the town of New Ulm and laying siege to nearby Fort Ridgley. Other Sioux joined the struggle, and violence erupted west to the Dakotas and south into Iowa. Soon some 800 whites

The Siege of New Ulm, painted in 1902 by H. August Schwabe
40 years after the Santee Sioux destroyed the Minnesota town

lay dead, only 100 of them soldiers. The Natives took hundreds
more as prisoners, and many faced an agonizing future that had
them wishing they were among the casualties.

It took a few weeks for the Americans to organize a response.
Governor Alexander Ramsey of Minnesota hired trader and one-
time colonel Henry H. Sibley to repel the assault. In late September,

Sibley eventually defeated Little Crow at Wood Lake, Minnesota. Four hundred Santee were brought before a commission to prove their innocence. Nearly 350 couldn't, and of these, some 300 were sentenced to hang.

Only President Lincoln's personal intervention introduced justice to the proceedings. Ignoring the public outcry in Minnesota, he personally reviewed the reports dealing with the condemned Santee. In the end, he decided that only 38 should die. On December 26, 1862, the sentence was carried out, and Minnesotans learned something of the courage of the Santee because the braves sang their death songs while the nooses were slipped around their necks. Those Santee who were not executed were dispossessed of their land and treaty rights and sent to a reservation in Nevada. Others, who had escaped Sibley's clutches, fled north to Canada or west to the Plains. The Teton Sioux took in many and learned from them what life was like with the Wasichus.

The Cheyenne, neighbors of the Teton Sioux to the southwest, also had problems with the white man. The Cheyenne had agreed to the terms of the 1851 Fort Laramie Treaty, but they discovered that government commitments meant little where settlers' and prospectors' interests were concerned. In the late 1850s, gold was discovered in the Front Range of the Rocky Mountains. Prospectors traveled the Smoky Hill Trail to get to the gold fields. The trail cut through Cheyenne territory south of the Platte River and was protected by the treaty. The Southern Cheyenne attacked the prospectors. In July 1857, Colonel Edwin Sumner then defeated the Cheyenne at the Battle of the Solomon River and brought a temporary end to Native aggression. Young Crazy Horse witnessed that battle.

But the prospectors kept coming. News of a gold strike along Clear Creek in the eastern foothills of the central Rocky Mountains (west of Denver) in 1859 encouraged thousands more to head west. A year later, prospectors were shouting, "Pike's Peak or Bust" as they made their way to the siver diggings west of Colorado City. Not

The December 1862 execution of 38 Santee Sioux convicted in the
Minnesota uprising. They sang death songs as they were hanged.

much gold was taken from Colorado during these early boom years.
The peak year of production was 1862 with only $3.4 million in gold
mined. By comparison, California's peak year of 1852 produced $81
million. Still, a gold rush takes on a life of its own, and word of a strike
was enough to infect men with gold fever, draw them west and dis-
rupt Native ways.

As the rush petered out, many miners decided to homestead in the region, and soon, increasing numbers of settlers joined them. Governor John Evans of Colorado was anxious to open land for the newcomers, and he set about negotiating with the local Cheyenne and Arapaho. Some Natives anticipated that they would inevitably lose their ancestral lands to the white man, and in an effort to protect some of it, they signed the Treaty of Fort Wise in 1861. The Natives ceded large amounts of land, agreeing to live on a reservation and allowing roads across their territory. Many Cheyenne were angry about the treaty and claimed that there had been bribery and misinformation about land cessions. They refused to abide by the treaty's terms, and by the summer of 1863, they were raiding everything that remotely suggested a white presence.

Events to the north further inflamed the dispute. In July 1864, General Alfred Sully and a 2220-strong army contingent crushed Inkpaduta's Santee Sioux at the Battle of Kildeer Mountain not far from Crazy Horse's home in the Powder River country. In response, incensed Sioux sent the war pipe to the Cheyenne and Arapaho asking them to join in a larger Native resistance. Headmen of those tribes declined. When Governor Evans learned of the Sioux effort, he labeled the rebellious local Natives as hostiles and ordered the militia, the Third Colorado Volunteers, into the field under the command of Colonel John Chivington.

Chivington was a military leader of some reputation, which he acquired mostly during the Civil War. As an officer in the Union Army, he had enjoyed success fighting Confederate forces. He was an arrogant man with his sights set on political office, all too aware that a decisive victory over the Natives could serve as a springboard for his political ambitions. The fact that he hated Natives only gave added pleasure to his mission. Chivington initiated his campaign against the Natives in the spring of 1864, attacking all he encountered, stealing possessions and razing villages. Natives retaliated by raiding white settlements. The result was the Cheyenne-Arapaho (Colorado) War. Governor Evans, increasingly determined to crush the Natives, issued a proclamation in August urging citizens to form themselves into parties to hunt them down. Evans' policies matched Chivington's own outlook. For months he had been telling the people of Colorado to kill every red man they saw.

The war took a grisly turn in the fall of 1864 when Chivington encountered Black Kettle's band of Cheyenne along the Sand Creek. Although some braves in Black Kettle's band had raided white settlements, Black Kettle was considered a "friendly," the term used for Natives who were at peace with the government. A few months previously he had even met with Governor Evans in an effort to negotiate peace terms. In the heat of battle, however, Evans saw no Natives as peaceful, and he rejected Black Kettle's overtures. Nevertheless, Black Kettle was determined to avoid violence, and he met with the commanding officer of Fort Lyon, who promised that the army would protect his band until peace was secured.

But Evans and Chivington shared a differing view. With the governor's approval, Chivington and the militia set out for Sand Creek in search of Black Kettle's band. Soldiers out of Fort Lyon joined them—a more belligerent officer had replaced the commanding officer who had agreed to protect Black Kettle. On the morning of November 29, a force in excess of 700 men surrounded Black Kettle's camp. Although the camp held a similar number, only 200 of them were warriors. When some of the lesser ranking army officers pointed out that Black Kettle believed his band to be under the protection of the army, Chivington declared that he had "come to kill Indians and believe it is right and honorable to use any means under God's heaven to kill Indians."

Aware that the situation was serious, Black Kettle raised both American and white flags over his tipi and then rushed to meet with Chivington. Black Kettle did not reach him before the colonel gave the order to fire. The attack continued for most of the day. The Cheyenne suffered 163 deaths, two-thirds of whom were women and children, while Chivington lost nine men. Among the dead was Yellow Woman, whom Crazy Horse had rescued some years before.

The scalps of many of the dead Natives were later displayed in Denver, where Chivington was fêted as a hero.

As news of the attack spread, however, most Americans were outraged. Chivington's offensive was soon dubbed the Sand Creek Massacre, and public pressure resulted in a congressional investigation. Testimony revealed the horror of the attack. Eyewitness Robert Bent, brother to a mixed-blood Cheyenne warrior, reported the grisly details:

I saw five squaws hiding under a bank. When the troops came up to them, they ran out and showed their persons to let the soldiers know they were squaws. They begged for mercy, but the soldiers shot them all. I saw a squaw lying on the bank, whose leg had been broken by a shell. A soldier came up to her with a drawn saber. She raised her arm to protect herself when he struck, breaking her arm; she rolled over and raised her other arm when he struck again, breaking it. Then he left her without killing her.

Some 30 or 40 squaws and children were hiding in a hole for protection. [They] sent out a little girl about six years old with a white flag on a stick. She was shot and killed and all the [others] in the hole were killed.

I saw one squaw cut open with her unborn child lying by her side. I saw the body of White Antelope [an elder headman] with his privates cut off, and I heard a soldier say he was going to make a tobacco pouch out of them. I saw one squaw whose privates had been cut out. I saw a little girl who had been hid in the sand. Two soldiers drew their pistols and shot her, then pulled her out of the sand by the arm. I saw quite a number of infants in arms killed along with their mothers.

The investigation was damning, and faced with a court-martial, Chivington resigned. But the damage was done. When word of the attack reached neighboring tribes, including Crazy Horse's band, there was not much debate about how best to deal with the Wasichus.

Most of the ragged survivors of Black Kettle's band found their way to a Cheyenne camp on the south fork of the Smoky Hill River. When the Cheyenne first saw their fellow tribe members injured, hungry and afraid, they were shocked. When they heard the story of the Sand Creek Massacre, they were outraged. Black Kettle's band had been promised sanctuary, yet they had still been attacked. Even those Cheyenne who did not harbor hatred for white men could only conclude that they were not to be trusted. The Cheyenne leaders held a council. Most of those present agreed that justice could only be gained with revenge; such was the Native way. Despite Black Kettle's objections, the council decided to go to war.

They sent out the war pipe to other Cheyenne bands and to their allies, the Sioux in the north and the Arapaho in the south. At first, many must have wondered why the pipe arrived during the Moon of the Popping Trees (December), with snow already blanketing ground, because the Natives rarely fought in the winter. But when the runners explained the situation, most were quick to ignore the season, smoke the pipe and commit themselves to war. By the time the Moon of Popping Trees had disappeared, about 800 Cheyenne, Oglala and Brulé Sioux and Northern Arapaho lodges had gathered just south of the Platte River on Cherry Creek, a tributary of the Republican River.

Crazy Horse was not among their number. Throughout most of 1864 he lived with Old Man Afraid's band in the Powder River country, where they remained mostly unaffected by the Wasichus. Although the northern Oglala were aware of the attacks on the Santee Sioux and of General Sibley's push into eastern Teton Sioux territory, they remained content to hunt and to fight their traditional Native enemies. Sometime in 1864, Old Man Afraid's band apparently subdivided, and a group of them moved south. Crazy Horse moved with them, but he still lived a considerable distance from the site of the Sand Creek Massacre, and he did not know of the war

Henry Sibley (1811–91) in 1850 as Minnesota's territorial governor; commander of the state militia during the 1862 Santee uprising

pipe until early 1865. When Crazy Horse learned of the cowardly attack on the Cheyenne, with whom he enjoyed a special relationship, he rode south immediately. By then, the combined force along Cherry Creek had already made their first successful strike.

In council at Cherry Creek, chiefs and headmen decided to attack Julesburg and nearby Camp Rankin (renamed Fort Sedgwick in September 1865), both on the South Platte River, just west of the Forks of the Platte. Julesburg was a stage station and Camp Rankin a one-company military post. Both were hated symbols of white intrusion. The Native plan was built around deception. The

Cheyenne leader Big Crow was to lead a small decoy party to attack Julesburg. The Natives anticipated that the commanding officer of Camp Rankin would send out soldiers to defend the settlement. The great body of Native warriors would then strike. Victory seemed assured.

Early in the Moon of Frost in the Tipi (January), 1000 warriors set out for Julesburg. Size alone ensured that the war party was not ordinary. It was also more formally organized than was usual for a war party. Those who planned the attack strategy, war chiefs and pipe bearers, rode at the front. They were followed by columns of warriors, who were kept in line by patrolling *akicita*, chosen from many different warriors' societies.

On the morning of January 7, Big Crow and six warriors sprang the trap. They rode past Camp Rankin, alerting the soldiers, and made for Julesburg. Rather than attack, the warriors circled the buildings, shouting war whoops and firing their rifles. As expected, Post Commander Captain Nicholas O'Brien led a force of 38 soldiers out of Camp Rankin to defend the settlement. As they approached the Natives, Big Crow ordered his warriors to fall back. O'Brien signaled his men to follow, and the soldiers and some settlers gave chase. The order was poorly considered because it did not take into account the terrain. The soldiers and settlers had to ride out of a gully and towards some nearby hills, which provided a perfect blind for the warriors. They had chosen their point of attack well.

The only weakness in the Native strategy was that warriors generally fought independently. While war chiefs made plans for battle, they did not assume an authority that demanded obedience from the warriors. In battle, a man was essentially free to do as he chose. Native warfare depended on notions of free spiritedness and individual courage. A warrior fought when he was ready and how he thought best. Older warriors generally did not have to prove their courage, and they had enough experience to avoid actions that might put an attack or a raid into jeopardy. But younger warriors were anxious to demonstrate their bravery, and a charge that allowed one to count first coup would go far towards achieving that end. As a result, young warriors often attacked before any signal was given.

As the Wasichus chased Big Crow and his decoy, some young warriors broke away from the restraining *akicita* and the main Native force hidden behind the hills. But they charged too soon, before the soldiers and settlers were in striking distance. Realizing that the element of surprise had been lost, the other warriors surged ahead to join the charge. O'Brien had just enough time to order a retreat, saving most of his party—14 soldiers and 4 settlers died before they reached Camp Rankin, and none of them were buried with their scalps. The stockade was an adequate barrier and prevented further bloodshed, although those inside spent an uneasy morning listening to the war whoops, thudding arrows and cracking gunfire of the many Natives who surrounded the camp.

Lieutenant Eugene Ware, holed up in Camp Rankin, described the sight from inside the barricade:

We could hear them shrieking and yelling, we could hear the tum-tum of a native drum, and we could hear a chorus of shouting. Then we could see them circling around the fire, then separately stamping the ground and making gestures.... We knew that the bottled liquors destined for Denver were beginning to do their work and a perfect orgy was ensuing. It kept up constantly. It seemed as if exhausted Indians fell back and let fresh ones take hold.

Aware that little was to be gained by continuing to pin down those at Camp Rankin, most of the warriors made for Julesburg, which had quickly been deserted. The many unburdened packhorses that the warriors had brought with them suggested that the sacking of the settlement was part of their original strategy. For the most part, they took food—flour, sugar and corn. The plunder was so great that it took three days to coax the overloaded packhorses back to the camp at Cherry Creek. The warriors celebrated with great enthusiasm and with great justification. They had taken revenge and an unimaginable amount of plunder, and no Native lives had been lost. Scalp dances, singing and feasting lasted well into the next day.

Following the victory, the war chiefs met in council. They were not yet satisfied and made plans to raid along the Platte River, where there was ample opportunity to strike along the California/Oregon Trail. In late January, they broke camp, and on the January 28, they began attacking along the South Platte River. They targeted stage stations, wagon trains and ranches, killing all the whites they found. The few soldiers in the region stayed in their forts, afraid to attack a Native village that had lodges stretching for four miles along the riverside. For weeks the Natives cut off all westerly access through the region.

Failure to take Camp Rankin was the one disappointing raid in early 1865. Determined warriors decided to try to take it again. This time Crazy Horse joined them; he was one of the few northern Sioux to participate in the Cheyenne-Arapaho War. With his friend Little Big Man, he joined in the raids along the South Platte. Crazy Horse's efforts demonstrated that his reputation as a warrior was deserved, so when the decision was made to attack Camp Rankin again, he led the decoy party. Early in the Moon of the Dark Red Calves (February), 1000 warriors gathered in the hills near Camp Rankin. Crazy Horse led a handful of warriors towards the stockade, but despite their best efforts to lure the soldiers out, they were unsuccessful. The soldiers had learned their lesson and were not about to fall for the same ploy twice. The warriors turned to Julesburg, raided it and destroyed the buildings.

Content with their victories, the bands dispersed. The Native way of warfare did not include any notion of fighting an enemy to the finish. Most Sioux headed north for the Powder River country. For a time they rode along the Overland Trail, which hugged the Medicine Bow Mountains, and continued to destroy any evidence of a white presence. Later that spring, after the warriors had left the

Little Big Man in 1877. He was Crazy Horse's close friend for many years and fought with him against the Wasichus.

region, army officials reported razed and desolate stretches in excess of 100 miles, including the destruction of a large section of the Overland Stage Line. While many warriors continued north, where they eventually showed wide-eyed band members great amounts of booty and belts heavy with scalps, Crazy Horse decided to ride for Crow territory west of the White Mountains (Bighorn Mountains). While he enjoyed the raiding, he tired of tearing down telegraph wires and burning Wasichu buildings. Crazy Horse longed for a real fight where a warrior could demonstrate his courage in personal combat.

It is not known whether he found any Crow to fight on this occasion, but by early summer he returned to the Oglala camp south of the Powder River country. When he arrived, he was informed that the Big Bellies, a small group of elder warriors, had called for a ceremony to install new shirt wearers, a position that Crazy Horse had long desired.

When the ceremony began, a select group mounted their horses and rode around the camp. Each time they completed a circle, they called the name of one chosen to be a shirt wearer. On the fourth and final pass, they shouted, "Crazy Horse!"

Some, including Crazy Horse, were surprised to hear his name. He was without the powerful relatives or alliances in the tribe that were the usual prerequisites to attaining the position. Crazy Horse knew that he had been selected because of his ability as a warrior. As he listened to the Big Bellies describe his responsibilities, Crazy Horse felt great satisfaction.

Following the ceremony of investiture, the war chiefs held council. Crazy Horse was present for the discussions, but he said little. It was clear that many were still angry about the attack at Kildeer Mountain and the Sand Creek Massacre. The council decided to launch another attack on the Wasichus. They sent the war pipe to other Sioux bands and to the Cheyenne and Arapaho. Crazy Horse joined some 3000 warriors near the Platte River in the Moon When the Cherries are Ripe (July). Their target was the Platte River Bridge, which crossed the North Platte River at what is now Casper, Wyoming. The bridge was well used by settlers traveling on the California/Oregon Trail, as well as by the military and freighters, and its importance was emphasized by the nearby army garrison stationed to protect it.

Crazy Horse led a small decoy party of 10 warriors to the bridge, anticipating that they would draw the soldiers out. The troop rode across the bridge with a cannon in tow. Crazy Horse directed the warriors to fall back towards the bluff that concealed the great body of warriors. Rather than pursue the decoy party, however, the soldiers set up their cannon and began firing. Despite the best efforts of the *akicita*, who had resorted to beating warriors anxious to see what the cannon fire was about, some of the younger warriors dashed forward, revealing the trap. The soldiers quickly retreated.

The soldiers might have remained in the garrison had a supply train not approached the next morning. A troop of cavalry rode out to escort them in. The warriors attacked, and in the face of the great number of the enemy, the soldiers broke formation and ran for the garrison. Less than half a dozen soldiers died, however, because few warriors had rifles, and most were unwilling to get too close to the soldiers, who were well armed, or to the cannon that protected them. The warriors then turned on the supply train. Unlike the soldiers, those with the supply train were still too far from the garrison to run for safety. They were also out of range of the garrison's cannons. Only one of the 25 men escaped.

The Natives lost 60 warriors, and they'd had their fill of fighting. The next day the bands dispersed, and Crazy Horse and his fellow Oglala headed back to the Powder River country.

〰〰〰

When they returned to the Powder River country, the Sioux hoped to slip back into the routine of daily life. It was the Moon of the Black Cherries (August), and it would soon be necessary to hunt buffalo for winter. In the meantime, the warriors wanted to relax because spring and early summer had seen many battles. But their desire for normalcy was not to be satisfied.

The American Civil War had come to a close, and troops were finally available to fight on the Plains. General Patrick Connor, who commanded the Military District of the Plains, was ordered to direct the Powder River Expedition against the Natives. The government wanted the territory opened and the Natives punished for their raiding and killing along the Platte River. Connor divided his 2500 men

General Patrick Connor (1820–91). He commanded the failed
Powder River Expedition of 1865 against the Plains Natives.

into three columns, which proved to be a questionable strategy. In
his one major encounter against the Arapaho, Connor's troops suffered many injuries without claiming victory. The Sioux and
Cheyenne effectively harassed the other columns. Crazy Horse
participated in a series of attacks on Colonel Nelson Cole's column
along the lower Powder River in early September. Few soldiers were
killed, but the Sioux were able to cut off supply lines, forcing the soldiers to kill their horses and mules for food.

By the end of September, the Powder River Expedition had
come to an inglorious close. The soldiers had taken a few ponies,

but the Native camps were full of supplies that had been intended for the United States Army. American government officials considered the campaign an expensive failure and one it could ill-afford with the financial drain of southern reconstruction after the Civil War. They were open to a new approach. Under additional pressure from politicians and religious organizations who believed that the attacks on the Plains Natives had been unwarranted (and who also wanted to "save" the Natives through religious and economic conversion), the federal government created the Northwest Treaty Commission. Led by Newton Edmunds, the governor of Dakota Territory, the commission was directed to negotiate peace treaties with the bands along the upper Missouri River. In October 1865, nine treaties were signed with Sioux bands. The Fort Sully treaties required that signatories cease hostilities against whites and other Natives, and that they steer clear of overland trails. In return the Natives received money and individual lots of land, if they wanted to settle down.

Most of the Sioux who "touched the pen" were those already dependent on the goodwill of the Wasichus for their survival. The more independent-minded Sioux, who continued to follow traditional ways, including those bands in the Powder River country and east to the Missouri River, were opposed to making treaty and they continued to raid south into Platte River country. These Sioux had major grievances they wanted settled before they contemplated peace. For the Oglala, those grievances centered on the Bozeman Trail.

The Bozeman Trail had its origin in the Montana gold strikes of the late 1850s and early 1860s. The original route into the region followed the Missouri River, but it was a cumbersome and time-consuming journey. Between 1863 and 1865, trader John Bozeman blazed a shortcut that connected the California/Oregon Trail with the gold fields. The trail ran from Fort Laramie, across the upper Powder River, along the eastern foothills of the Bighorn Mountains to the Yellowstone River, finally ending at Virginia City in Montana Territory. While prospectors had set their sights on gold, the Sioux

feared that the Wasichus wanted the Powder River country for settlement, hence the Oglala raids along the Platte River.

Late in 1865, Colonel Henry Maynadier, commanding officer at
Fort Laramie, was directed by his superiors to send a copy of the
treaty recently signed by the Laramie Loafers to the Powder River
Sioux. But no soldier had the courage to carry it north. It wasn't
until year's end that one of the Loafers was persuaded to deliver the
document. Predictably, the northern Sioux were not interested, but
after a particularly hard winter, word arrived at Fort Laramie that
the Oglala leaders were willing to talk. A pleased E.B. Taylor, head
of the commission appointed by President Johnson to negotiate
with the Teton Sioux, hurried to Fort Laramie. He sent gifts to the
Oglala with a message that the American government also wanted
a peace council. Led by Red Cloud and Old Man Afraid, the Oglala
arrived at Fort Laramie in June 1866. Crazy Horse was with them.

The council started well. Oglala leaders demanded that the treaty
be explained to them in great detail, and a hopeful Taylor enthusiastically obliged. The Natives said little until Taylor reached the clause
concerning the construction of roads through the Powder River
country. Red Cloud then raised his hand.

"We will never sign such a treaty," he declared.

"The government isn't really interested in building new roads
through the Powder River country," noted Taylor. "The government
wants only to be assured that it can maintain the Bozeman Trail."

"It is bad enough," answered Red Cloud, who then called for an
end to the day's discussion so that the Oglala might confer.

The Oglala left the fort and returned to their camp. While they
smoked their pipes and talked about the Wasichu's treaty, news
arrived that threw the council into chaos. Standing Elk, a known
government friendly whose sudden appearance at the council was
questioned by some, brought the news.

"You may not care for my position," he declared, "but you will
want to know what I have seen."

"Let him speak," said Old Man Afraid.

"A few days ago I saw many Wasichus marching up the North Platte River. When they camped, I entered and spoke to their chief. He told me that they were going to the Powder River to build forts and to guard the Bozeman Trail," revealed Standing Elk.

He was correct. In April, Colonel Henry B. Carrington, in charge of the newly organized Department of the Platte, had been authorized to take an army battalion (some 700 soldiers) to the Bozeman Trail. He was to oversee the trail's development and to protect those who traveled on it, which meant the construction of forts.

The Oglala were incensed. When the peace council reconvened, Taylor knew he was in for trouble.

"Standing Elk has told us that the Wasichus march along the Bozeman Trail," said Young Man Afraid. "I hope he is mistaken. If the Wasichus go into the Powder River country, in two moons the command would not have a hoof left."

"They are not there to cause trouble," replied Taylor. "They are there to protect the right of way for settlers."

Red Cloud leapt up upon hearing Taylor's response.

"In this and Wakan Tanka I trust for the right," he shouted while holding his rifle high for all to see. He then walked from the council arena, a symbolic act indicating he would no longer be part of any relationship with the commissioners. He sat on the floor, wrapping himself in his blanket and refusing to talk to Taylor, who was anxious to explain his government's position.

Finally, Red Cloud shouted over him. "The Great Father sends us presents and wants us to sell him the road, but White Chief goes with Wasichus to steal the road before the Indians can say yes or no. I will take no gifts. You treat us as children, pretending to negotiate for a country you have already taken by force. My people called these plains home," stretching his arm from beneath his blanket and making an arc with it. "You have forced us north. We are crowded around the Powder River. There is not enough buffalo to feed us. Our women and children starve."

Then Red Cloud turned to the Sioux.

"It is better to fight. What else is there? To starve? To die in a land no longer ours? We should fight and we will win."

Red Cloud quickly left Fort Laramie with those who supported him and his strong words, including Crazy Horse. While some friendlies—including the Brulé chief Spotted Tail—made treaty, the commission was in a shambles. Ironically, the United States Senate subsequently rejected the treaty, but the Natives were not informed.

Red Cloud headed for the Powder River country, but he was in no hurry to get there. He intended to act on his words and force the Wasichus from the Bozeman Trail. On July 17, Red Cloud's warriors raided the site chosen for Fort Phil Kearny, at the forks of the Big Piney and Little Piney creeks, fewer than 50 miles from the Powder River. Construction had only started the week before, and with the sudden raid, Colonel Carrington realized that the Sioux were watching his every move. The Sioux stole easily 200 horses and mules in a raid that marked the beginning of what has become known as Red Cloud's War. A week later, they attacked three wagon trains bound for Montana. Carrington sent out soldiers to assist the migrants, but Red Cloud attacked them as well.

Carrington grew so concerned about Red Cloud's offensive that he tried to send word to the Oglala chief to seek a peace council. Whether Red Cloud received the message is unknown, but he was not interested in peace unless the Wasichus were removed. Only then would Sioux hunting territory be safe, and with that, their traditional way of life. Carrington couldn't insure that. And it appeared to the Oglala that the Wasichus were more determined than ever to control the Bozeman Trail. In August, they began construction on Fort C.F. Smith, located on the Bighorn River. Including Fort Reno, which had been built by General Connor during the disastrous Powder River expedition in 1865, three forts had been built along the Bozeman Trail. That was three too many for the Oglala.

Some warriors, including Crazy Horse, continued to raid throughout the late summer. Meanwhile, the Oglala held a Sun Dance along the Tongue River. They decided to send the war pipe to neighboring tribes. Many smoked it, and by November, Red Cloud looked with satisfaction at the large number—3000 Sioux, Cheyenne and Arapaho—gathered in his camp. He sent warriors out to harass Fort Phil Kearny until it was under a state of constant siege. And more trouble occurred along the Bozeman Trail. Between August and December, Natives killed more than 150 soldiers and travelers and stole over 700 animals. Sioux confidence grew with the success of their raids. They talked of taking the fort. Crazy Horse met with Red Cloud, Hump and other shirt wearers to discuss the matter.

"Our warriors greatly outnumber the Wasichus," observed Hump.

"The problem isn't numbers," replied Red Cloud. "It is weapons. All the Wasichus have rifles, while we have but a few. It is impossible to take the fort while they can so easily fire at our braves from behind shelter."

"Then we must draw them out into the open," suggested Crazy Horse. "We might remain hidden and allow our arrows to rain down upon them. They will bring death as surely as bullets. Those not killed will feel the crushing blow of our war clubs."

They agreed and made plans to lure out a detachment of soldiers from Fort Phil Kearny to ambush them. The Oglala knew that the fort was dependent on woodcutters to supply it with firewood. They expected that a small band of warriors could pin down the wood train, and the fort commander would send out soldiers to support it. The great body of warriors would remain hidden until the detachment arrived; then they would attack. It was an old Native war strategy, effective because most of their many raids never included more than a few dozen warriors.

On December 6, Crazy Horse remained with the ambush party and watched from a bluff as the plan was put into action. As anticipated, the decoy party pinned down the woodcutters and drew out a detachment of some 40 soldiers. A second detachment, led by Carrington himself, rode out to attack the Oglala, whom they expected to flee as they usually did. The situation quickly

deteriorated. The decoy closed too quickly on the first detach-
ment, and the ambushers turned on the second detachment
before the soldiers were close enough to be attacked effectively.
Carrington realized what was happening and called a hasty retreat.
The Oglala took only two lives, and the attack was a failure. Crazy
Horse was enraged.

"We cannot expect victory if the warriors cannot hold their places
until it is time to attack! The warriors want to count coup, but that
will not remove the Wasichus," he declared to Hump. Crazy Horse's
anger over the incident was understandable but he could hardly hold
the warriors responsible. They had fought as they always had,
responsible for their own actions and anxious to demonstrate their
bravery by counting coup. Crazy Horse realized that fighting the
Wasichus required a new approach. But he was no orator, and he
asked Hump to take his message to council.

"Make sure that everyone understands what is necessary. Success
will not come in fighting as we always have."

Red Cloud was anxious to attack again, so he listened willingly to
Crazy Horse's observations. Perhaps Crazy Horse's new standing
among the Oglala also influenced Red Cloud. The older, more
responsible men of the tribe had made Crazy Horse war chief of
the whole Oglala tribe. However, it is unlikely that his authority
exceeded Red Cloud's.

The council decided again to try the strategy used on December 6.
This time, however, Red Cloud wanted there to be no escape for the
Wasichus, so the ambush party was increased from 300 to 2000 warriors. Crazy Horse would lead the decoy party while Hump was
responsible for the ambush party, which would be hidden in a ravine
along Peno Creek, a few miles from the fort.

On December 20, the evening before the planned attack, Red
Cloud and the shirt wearers called on a *wintke*, who had special
powers, to seek a vision of the battle. He pulled a blanket over his
head and rode away towards a hill, tooting on a bone whistle. He
soon returned.

Oglala chief Red Cloud (1821–1909). Red Cloud was among the most prominent Natives during the Plains warfare of the 1860s. He opposed the construction of the Bozeman Trail through Sioux hunting grounds in the Powder River country. When the United States government built a series of forts along the route to protect travelers, Red Cloud led a widespread Native resistance known as Red Cloud's War. When it was over, the army had abandoned its posts, a decisive victory for the Sioux. Red Cloud signed the 1868 Fort Laramie Treaty and was made chief of his own agency near Camp Robinson. When Crazy Horse surrendered, Red Cloud feared that Crazy Horse's popularity might challenge his influence among reservation Sioux and army authorities, and he conspired against his one-time ally.

"I have 10 men, 5 in each hand. Do you want them?" he asked.

"No, we do not wish them," replied the shirt wearers. "Look at all these people here. Do you think that 10 men are enough to go around?"

The *wintke* rode away again. When he came back, his horse making a slow trot, he had different news.

"I have 10 men in each hand, 20 in all. Do you wish them?"

"No," replied Red Cloud. "They are not enough."

The *wintke* sighed and departed. He urged his horse to run fast when he next returned.

"I have 20 men in one hand and 30 in the other," he said. "The 30 are in the hand on the side towards which I am leaning."

Yet again the shirt wearers shook their heads. The *wintke* heeled his horse and left. When he returned, his pony rode so fast that it kicked up a cloud of dust. He pulled the animal to a stop and fell to the ground, striking it with both hands.

"Answer me quickly," he gasped. "I have 100 or more."

Led by Red Cloud, the shirt wearers shouted enthusiastically. They wanted a favorable vision, and the *wintke* had finally delivered it. He had seen that the warriors would take the scalps of 100 Wasichus! Their confidence increased.

The next day fortune, or perhaps Wakan Tanka, smiled on the Oglala. Carrington dispatched Captain William Fetterman to relieve the woodcutters. Fetterman was another braggart ignorant of the strength and ability of the Sioux. All he needed, he often declared, was a company of cavalry to wipe out 1000 Sioux. When he approached the woodcutters with his command of 80 men, the Oglala decoy party led by Crazy Horse fell back. Although he was under strict orders from Carrington not to pursue for fear of ambush, Fetterman believed retreat to be both unnecessary and cowardly. As he watched the Sioux scamper back to Lodge Trail Ridge, he knew he was gaining on them. He didn't question why pursuit was so easy. Instead, he smiled. Victory would be his, and promotion was sure to follow.

Crazy Horse was smiling as well. Hump and the *akicita* had managed to contain the warriors and remain concealed. When the

An illustration of the Fetterman Massacre from *Harper's Weekly*, March 1867; known by the Sioux as the Battle of 100 Killed

decoy party reached the ravine, 2000 warriors suddenly joined them. Fetterman could not retreat. The short battle was chaotic.

Black Elk, not yet a warrior, said, "There were many bullets but there were more arrows—so many that it was like a cloud of grasshoppers all above and around the Wasichus; and our people shooting around shot each other."

The detachment was wiped out, and 13 warriors also died. Americans came to know the battle as the Fetterman Massacre, but the Sioux called it the Fight of 100 Killed (they believed that they had killed 100 Wasichus). Under either name, it was the greatest defeat yet suffered by the cavalry.

It was also a grisly one, as Carrington describes, "Eyes torn out and laid on rocks; noses cut off; ears cut off; chins hewn off; teeth chopped out; joints of fingers, brains taken out and placed on rocks; entrails taken out and exposed; hands cut off; feet cut off; arms taken out from sockets; private parts severed and indecently placed on the person; eyes, ears, mouth and arms penetrated with spear-heads, sticks and arrows; ribs slashed to separation with knives; skulls severed in every form, from chin to crown; muscles of calves, thighs, stomach, breast, back, arms and cheeks taken out. Punctures on every sensitive part of the body, even to the soles of the feet and palms of the hand."

Neither Crazy Horse nor Hump participated in the butchery. A white scout reported that they both left the battlefield after the victory. They went in search of their old friend Lone Bear, who had disappeared during the fight. They found him so badly wounded that he could not move. He died in Crazy Horse's arms.

〰〰〰

After the Battle of 100 Killed, the warriors returned to their winter camps. Crazy Horse left for the Powder River country. Before the snow melted, however, he rode south with his brother Little Hawk, and they renewed their raiding along the southern Bozeman Trail. As spring gave way to summer, Crazy Horse was on his way back to the Powder River. There was to be a Sun Dance, and while Crazy Horse wasn't much interested in that, he knew that battle plans for summer would be discussed. Crazy Horse's voice would be needed.

When the Sun Dance was completed, the headmen met in council. Attending were Old Man Afraid, leader of the Big Bellies and an opponent of war, and Red Cloud, the ranking war chief. The council

dissolved into a heated dispute. The Big Bellies, respected village elders, desired peace, while the war chiefs and shirt wearers thought that
war was the only answer. Discussion reached a fever pitch when
unexpected news arrived at the council: the American government
wanted to make treaty. While the Sioux did not know it, their attacks
had forced the government's hand. Settlers were increasingly reluctant to go west, and those who did complained about Sioux harassment. Railroad expansion, which had taken on a full head of steam
after the Civil War, was threatened. It was costly to send troops that
might offer protection. And soldiers weren't readily available because
about half of the American army was stationed in the south to ensure
a smooth transition to peace following the Civil War. Finally, in the
East, an increasingly loud clamor erupted that America's problems
with the Natives reflected official intolerance. To appease all factions,
the government dispatched additional troops to Fort Phil Kearny and
a peace commission to Fort Laramie.

"There is a season when the flower buds and one when the lake
freezes over," said Old Man Afraid. "There is also a season for peace,
and it has arrived."

"I have lived many years," replied Red Cloud, "and I have seen
much of the country. I have yet to see such a season. Brothers, we
have yet to lose a battle. Our camps are filled with the supplies our
warriors take in raids. We have more rifles than we've ever possessed.
And the Wasichus still threaten along the Bozeman Trail. Why
would we make peace?"

"We have rifles but no bullets," said one of the Big Bellies. "Rifles
without bullets aren't likely to bring victory."

"I have heard stories of the Wasichus battles in their big fight to
the east and south," added Old Man Afraid. "It is said that many
hundreds were left dead after the rifles fell silent. Do we want that?"

"Tales told by the Loafers to make themselves feel better," scoffed
Red Cloud. "Even if true, there is no warrior who would not fight
because he fears death."

His comment brought shouts of approval from the shirt wearers.

"They offer us money if we stop fighting and give them our land. I do not need money. Wakan Tanka provides for me," added Red Cloud.

"Already the buffalo disappear, brother," said Old Man Afraid. "Perhaps money is the new way that Wakan Tanka will provide for us. Is peace so bad?"

"No," interjected Crazy Horse, "peace is not so bad." All heads turned to him in surprise, anxious to hear what the warrior who so rarely spoke might say. "But this is not about peace. I have thought long about the Wasichus and what they want. Their demands will make us different and it will not be a good different. I do not want to be the last Sioux warrior. Without the land, that fate is certain."

"Change is certain," replied Old Man Afraid. "It always has been, and the wish of a warrior, even one so great as Crazy Horse, is not likely to make a difference. We should at least listen to what the Wasichus have to say."

"I don't want it said that my ears are closed," said Red Cloud. "We should listen. But if the words are not what we want to hear, then…" He raised his clenched fist.

It was decided that Old Man Afraid would go to Fort Laramie to listen to the Wasichus' proposal. But, at the insistence of the shirt wearers, he was not allowed to sign anything until the Wasichus abandoned the forts along the Bozeman Trail. In addition, Old Man Afraid was to ask the Wasichus for ammunition. He arrived at Fort Laramie in June. His request for ammunition, which he said would be used for hunting, was met with suspicion and, ultimately, rejection. Old Man Afraid left the fort without a peace agreement.

Crazy Horse was neither surprised nor disappointed with the outcome of Old Man Afraid's council. He joined other warriors in harassing wagon trains and soldiers on the Bozeman Trail, but it no longer brought satisfaction. Western-bound settlers had all but abandoned the trail, and the soldiers were increasingly cautious about venturing from the safety of their forts, so the warriors tired of raids that brought little return. In mid-summer 1867, Red Cloud sent runners to the tribes and bands that had dispersed over the winter, and many came to meet in council. Red Cloud found himself pressed to launch a substantial attack, but others disagreed about the target. The Cheyenne decided to attack Fort C.F. Smith, while the Sioux chose Fort Phil Kearny.

Crazy Horse, Hump and Red Cloud developed the Sioux battle plan. Previous raids on the fort had provided them with important information regarding its operation. Woodcutters worked near the Bighorn Mountains and were protected by a 26-man cavalry detachment camped about a mile away. Again, the Sioux planned to use a decoy. They would attack the detachment and draw out the soldiers. It appeared easy because the detachment camp was not fortified. Unknown to the Sioux, however, the soldiers were armed with new, superior weapons—breech-loading Springfield rifles— and their commanding officer, Captain J.N. Powell, was fast and creative under fire.

Crazy Horse led the decoy against the Wasichus on the morning of August 2, 1867. Powell took no chances, and when he spotted the first Sioux, he ordered his men to hurry to the woodcutters' location. The Sioux weren't even close to the target when the weakness of Sioux warfare again undermined the attack. A soldier fired on Crazy Horse, and the hidden Sioux broke ranks. Soon all 800 flooded onto the tree-cleared space around the Wasichus. Powell quickly ordered his men to arrange the woodcutters' wagon boxes in a circle.

With the element of surprise lost, Crazy Horse modified his plans. He had his braves circle the soldiers' position, an unusual approach for the Sioux to take. They would draw the soldiers' fire until their ammunition was depleted and then attack. However, the Sioux could not get close because of the high-powered rifles, and their arrows were unable to do more than lodge in the wooden wagon boxes. Crazy Horse led a few charges on the soldiers' position, but each time the soldiers repelled the Sioux. Six warriors died before Crazy Horse called a retreat. They had killed 10 Wasichus and taken many ponies, but it was not much of a victory. The Wagon

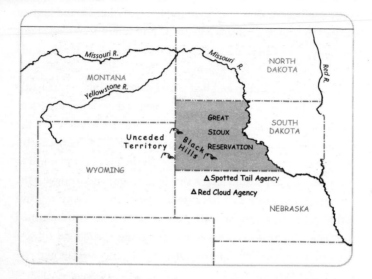

Box Fight, as the incident became known, taught Crazy Horse an important lesson, and he would never again attack Wasichus when they enjoyed a fortified position.

As the weeks passed, it seemed that Crazy Horse would no longer need to trouble himself over battle strategy. The Sioux and their allies had proven stubborn and certainly worthier adversaries than the United States government had expected. Despite massive expenditures, the cavalry was making little headway in bringing the Plains Natives under control. Concluding that the cost of waging war was too great, the government sent commissioners to Fort Laramie in the fall of 1867 to negotiate a peace settlement. Red Cloud, who always liked to keep government officials guessing, was far too preoccupied with the buffalo hunt to meet with them. They returned to Washington without a treaty.

The commissioners arrived again the following spring, and they agreed to Red Cloud's every demand. The Fort Laramie Treaty of 1868 pledged that the Bozeman Trail would be closed and the forts along it abandoned. The treaty also created the Great Sioux Reservation,

Articles of a Treaty made and concluded by and between Lieutenant General William T. Sherman, General William S. Harney, General Alfred H. Terry, General C. C. Augur, J. B. Henderson, Nathaniel G. Taylor, John B. Sanborn and Samuel F. Tappan, duly appointed Commissioners on the part of the *United States* and the different Bands of the *Sioux Nation of Indians* by their Chiefs and Head men whose names are hereto subscribed, they being duly authorized to act in the premises.

Article I. From this day forward all war between the parties to this agreement shall forever cease. The Government of the United States desires peace and its honor is hereby pledged to keep it. The Indians desire peace and they now pledge their honor to maintain it.

If bad men among the whites or among other people, subject to the authority of the United States, shall commit any wrong upon the person or property of the Indians, the United States will, upon proof, made to the Agent, and forwarded to the Commissioner of Indian Affairs at Washington City, proceed at once to cause the offender to be arrested and punished according to the laws of the United States and also reimburse the injured person for the loss sustained.

If bad men among the Indians shall commit a wrong or depredation upon the person or property of any one, white, black or Indian, subject to the authority of the United States and at peace therewith, the Indians herein named, solemnly agree that they

First page of the 1868 Fort Laramie Treaty, which created the Great Sioux Reservation and closed forts on the Bozeman Trail between the respective parties hereto, so far as such treaties and agreements obligate the United States to arm and provide money, clothing or other articles of property to such Indians and Bands of Indians as become parties to this Treaty, but no further.

In Testimony of all which we the said Commissioners and we the Chiefs and Head men of the Brulé Band of the Sioux Nation have hereunto set our hands and seals at Fort Laramie, Dakota Territory this twenty-ninth day of April in the year one thousand eight hundred and sixty eight.

N. G. Taylor   (seal)
W. T. Sherman   (seal)
Wm. S. Harney
Bvt. Maj. Gen. U.S.A.   (seal)

John B. Sanborn   (seal)
S. F. Tappan   (seal)
C. C. Augur   (seal)
Bvt. Maj. Gen.
Alfred H. Terry   (seal)
                        (seal)

Attest
A. S. H. White,
Secretary.

The last page of the 1868 Fort Laramie Treaty signed by the commissioners who negotiated it which included much of northern Wyoming and the Black Hills. White settlers and travelers were forbidden access to the region although officials on government business were permitted a right of way. It was an amazing victory for the Sioux and their allies, and they celebrated by burning down the empty Forts C.F. Smith and Reno.

Crazy Horse was not at the peace council in November when Red Cloud "touched the pen." He had no reason to be. As a warrior, his job was done; others could negotiate terms. While Crazy Horse would have refused to sign the treaty, he was pleased to rid the Powder River country of the Wasichus and was satisfied with his role in achieving it. He was less pleased with the decision of Red Cloud and Old Man Afraid to move to an agency near Fort Laramie. Crazy Horse was one of the few leaders who remained in the northern country, where throughout 1869 and 1870 he led the occasional raid on the Crow and the Shoshone. One battle, however, brought great tragedy into Crazy Horse's life.

In the fall of 1870, Crazy Horse joined Hump in a raid against the Shoshone. They made camp at the Wind River, and while the pair set out to scout the enemy camp, the cold rain that had dogged their journey turned to snow. Crazy Horse, ever cautious, felt that conditions were not right for fighting.

"I wonder if we can make it back to Cone Creek. I doubt if our horses can stand a fight in this slush. They sink in over their ankles," observed Crazy Horse. "It is best to head back to camp."

Hump would have none of it.

"You called off a fight here before, and when we got back to camp, they laughed at us. You and I have our good names to think about," Hump reminded him. "If you don't care about it, you can go back. I am going to stay here and fight."

"All right, we fight, if you feel that way about it," sighed Crazy Horse. "But we're going to get a good licking. You have a good gun, and I have a good gun, but look at our men! None has good guns, and most have only bows and arrows. It's a bad place for a fight and a bad day for it, and the enemy are 12 to our one."

The fight that followed quickly deteriorated for the Oglala. Sensing defeat, most of the warriors withdrew, leaving only Crazy Horse, Hump and Good Weasel to fight. They were having a hard time but they would not retreat. Amidst the rifle fire, Crazy Horse looked over at Hump and saw that his horse was limping.

"We're done for," shouted Hump over the din. "My horse has a wound in the leg."

"I know it!" answered Crazy Horse. "We were up against it from the beginning."

Crazy Horse called his war cry, and it was echoed quickly by Hump. The two charged the Shoshone. When Crazy Horse turned to look, he saw only Hump's pony. He saw the enemy swarm over the body of his *kola*. Hump was dead.

Red Feather, who had been a member of the war party, said that Crazy Horse returned to bury his close friend. All he found were bones. The coyotes had eaten the flesh. The Shoshone hadn't touched the remains. "When they found out whom they had killed, they beat it," noted Red Feather.

Distraught, Crazy Horse returned to the Powder River country, where more bad news awaited him. His brother Little Hawk had been killed while on a war expedition south of the Platte River. Crazy Horse was particularly close to his brother and had watched his growth as a man and a warrior with satisfaction.

Their mutual friend He Dog thought Little Hawk too rash, but he also remembered, "The old men claim…Little Hawk would have been a greater man than his brother Crazy Horse."

Within a few months, Crazy Horse had lost two of his closest friends. He felt more alone than ever.

〜〜〜

Crazy Horse walked through the Oglala camp near the northern extent of the Powder River Ridge, just east of the river that was its namesake. The camp was larger than it had been throughout the winter, as groups from the Red Cloud Agency traveled north for the summer as was their habit. Crazy Horse moved through the camp with little purpose, and as usual, villagers ignored him, perhaps because they were a bit afraid of him. Black Elk, who lived with him at the time, elaborated and speculated on this aspect of Crazy Horse's personality. "I was not afraid that he would hurt me; I was just afraid. Everybody felt that way about him, for he was a queer man and would go about the village without noticing people or saying anything. In his own teepee he would joke, and when he was on the warpath with a small party, he would joke to make his warriors feel good. But around the village he hardly noticed anybody, except little children. All the Lakotas like to dance and sing; but he never joined a dance, and they say nobody ever heard him sing. But everybody liked him, and they would do anything he wanted or go anywhere he said....He was a queer man. Maybe he was always part way into that world of his vision."

On one occasion, Crazy Horse's wanderings took him near the lodge of Black Buffalo Woman. He watched as she went about her afternoon chores, scraping a robe, stirring a pot. Although she was busy, Black Buffalo Woman still tended to the youngest of her three children, who was recently freed from the cradleboard and scampered about her mother's feet with glee. Crazy Horse smiled, and as he stood there, he realized that he often found himself near Black Buffalo Woman's lodge these days. He began to wonder if some unsuspected design was guiding his aimless walks. It was true that the sun traveled more quickly to its lodge when he watched Black Buffalo Woman. That was a welcome change because the days had seemed so long in the months since the passing of his *kola*.

Crazy Horse, who was always given to reflection, had done much thinking about the woman he had once loved. He could no longer pretend that his desire for her had disappeared. With that realization, he was no longer content with distant glances at Black Buffalo Woman. He grew bolder. He spoke to her and took her gifts, including a collection of elk teeth for a dress decoration. Others

Red Cloud Agency in 1876. Red Cloud settled at the agency near Camp Robinson after signing the 1868 Fort Laramie Treaty.

grew concerned about his unseemly behavior, and some men visited Worm, Crazy Horse's father, to warn him that trouble would come of Crazy Horse's actions. If his father relayed the warnings to Crazy Horse, they made no difference to him. He would not be satisfied until Black Buffalo Woman was his.

Crazy Horse never revealed why he made such an important decision at this time, but it is not difficult to surmise. His reputation as a warrior was secure. He could do nothing more—he could make no coups—nor could he attain positions that would cause others to speak his name with any greater respect. The Wasichus were defeated, and the recently signed Fort Laramie Treaty and the closure of the Bozeman Trail seemed to offer protection to the Powder River country. His intimate circle of friends was no more. Hump, Little Hawk and Lone Bear were gone. If he was to form a new relationship, there seemed no better time.

Crazy Horse was not concerned that he set his sights on a married woman. A woman who lived with a man (the Sioux had no word for wife) was his property, but the Sioux recognized the right of either party to end the relationship. A man might give away, throw away or mutilate his wife if she committed adultery or some other disgraceful act. A woman could end a relationship by throwing the man's belongings out of the lodge or simply by leaving. If it was decided (usually by friends) that her reasons for leaving were inadequate, she would have to return. If she remained determined to leave him, she would have to flee or be taken in by a man more powerful than her previous man. No, Crazy Horse was not concerned that Black Buffalo Woman was a taken woman. But he knew that her husband, No Water, was a jealous man unlikely to accept Black Buffalo Woman's departure.

Black Buffalo Woman told Crazy Horse as much when he proposed she come to his lodge.

"I will come with you, Crazy Horse," she agreed, "but we cannot stay in this camp. No Water would not stand for it. He would rather die than see me live with another man."

"Then we will go from this place," replied Crazy Horse.

He was not afraid of fighting No Water for Black Buffalo Woman, but he realized that No Water's objections would, at the very least, result in their being ostracized in the village. It was not a concern for him, but he did not want Black Buffalo Woman to suffer.

"I will make the plans. Be ready in three days. It will be easier if we do not have to take the children with us," he suggested.

Crazy Horse spread word that he was planning a raid against the Crow. Many wanted to join the small party he proposed, and he selected those he considered most loyal. Black Buffalo Woman made arrangements to have her children stay with friends. When the war party set out, Crazy Horse stopped at Black Buffalo Woman's lodge, and they rode north for the Yellowstone River.

No Water was aware of the Crazy Horse's recent attention to Black Buffalo Woman, and when she disappeared he guessed what had happened. No Water's friends informed him that the medicine man Chips had given Crazy Horse a love charm to induce her to leave with him. This made sense to No Water because he could think of no other reason why she would leave him. No Water's friends confronted Chips, who denied any involvement. When they threatened to kill Chips, he left the camp and stayed away for many months.

Chips was fortunate that No Water did not come seeking an explanation. But No Water was intent on getting revenge, and he set out immediately with a small war party of his own in search of Crazy Horse. He rode on a fast mule and carried a borrowed revolver. He was determined to use the weapon. Within two days, he found Crazy Horse camped with several other bands near where the Powder River forks from the Yellowstone River. Identifying Crazy Horse's teepee, he didn't delay in carrying out his bloody mission.

No Water burst into the lodge, cocked revolver in hand.

"I have come!" snarled No Water.

Crazy Horse jumped for his knife, but before he could grab it, No Water fired. The bullet struck just below the left nostril. Crazy Horse fell forward into the small fire.

Ignoring Black Buffalo Woman, who lifted some pegs and slipped out the back, No Water leapt from the lodge, proclaiming, "I have killed Crazy Horse."

He was treated to much rejoicing when he rejoined his friends. To kill such a warrior!

But Crazy Horse was not dead. The bullet followed the line of his teeth and caused only a fractured upper jaw. Word that Crazy Horse still lived soon reached No Water. He fled the camp when he learned that his enemy's friends were out to get him. They found only his mule, which they killed.

No Water went to his brother Black Twin, who promised protection. Meanwhile, Crazy Horse's friends carried him to the camp of his uncle Spotted Crow. He was in no condition to seek revenge, but his friends were anxious to ride against No Water. For a time, it seemed that more blood would be spilled, but the headmen of Spotted Crow's camp counseled peace. Those with No Water were glad to hear it, and soon three of No Water's quality ponies were delivered to Crazy Horse to atone for his act. They were accepted. Black Buffalo Woman, who had gone to live with her relatives, also returned to No Water. Crazy Horse insisted, however, that she not be punished. No Water agreed, although it was within his right to do to her as he wished.

Had it been an ordinary man who took Black Buffalo Woman, raised eyebrows, gossip and an exchange of property might well have been the end of it. But Crazy Horse was a shirt wearer, and he was held to a higher standard of conduct than others. The Big Bellies met to discuss what Crazy Horse had done. They decided that his actions were disruptive and not to the benefit of the community. He was an adulterer and no longer an example of a proper Sioux warrior. The Big Bellies agreed that Crazy Horse had broken his oath, and they asked him to return his shirt. Fourteen armed Short Hairs, who were responsible for the ceremonial shirt, arrived at his lodge demanding that he surrender his position.

The office of the shirt wearer suffered irreparable damage because of these events. He Dog recalled, "The shirt was never given to anybody else. Everything seemed to stop right there. Everything began to fall to pieces. After that it seemed as if anybody who wanted to could wear the shirt. It meant nothing."

While there is no record of how Crazy Horse felt about his public disgrace, he was humiliated and devastated. His actions demonstrated a failure to follow one of the Sioux cardinal rules, especially for a leader: Crazy Horse had put his own interests before the community's. One ill-advised choice had undermined a lifetime of effort dedicated to becoming the greatest warrior of his people. He had reached the top of that mountain only to be knocked off by a desire that he could not subdue. His lack of self-control may have been the greatest indignity.

Rightly or not, Crazy Horse never forgave No Water for shooting him. Some months later, a few bands were hunting buffalo near the mouth of the Bighorn River just north of the Yellowstone River. Both Crazy Horse and No Water were there, but neither knew of the other's presence. One afternoon, No Water spotted Crazy Horse approaching him. No Water grabbed the closest horse and rode quickly for the open prairie. Moccasin Top, who owned the horse and who was dressing his kill nearby, stood and scratched his head in confusion. Why would No Water take his horse? He was still wondering when Crazy Horse arrived.

"If you are here, then who was that man who just rode off on your buckskin horse?" he asked.

"That was No Water," replied Moccasin Top.

"I wish I had known it!" exclaimed Crazy Horse. "I would certainly have given him a bullet in return for the one he gave me."

Crazy Horse threw his hunting gear on the ground, gave his pony a strong kick with his heel and set out in pursuit of No Water. He gained on No Water and was close enough to see him plunge his horse into the Yellowstone River to cross it. Crazy Horse stopped at the river. Crazy Horse likely never saw No Water again because No Water soon left the northern Oglala to live with the Laramie Loafers at the Red Cloud Agency. Apparently Black Buffalo Woman joined him. Soon she had a daughter whose most distinguished traits were her light hair and complexion. Rumors circulated that she was Crazy Horse's child. No one ever knew for certain.

Crazy Horse also had children. He Dog was worried about his friend so he arranged a Cheyenne woman named Black Shawl for him. Crazy Horse probably knew the 28-year-old woman because he had ridden in battle with her brother Red Feather. Still, he was not interested in the match.

He sent his stepmother to Black Shawl's village asking her to relay a message to Black Shawl: "You must say there will be little joy in a life with me."

Black Shawl was not to be dissuaded. She gave Crazy Horse's stepmother a pair of moccasins beaded with a lightning bolt, reminiscent of the design he painted on his face during battle. The pair married in early 1871. In the fall, Black Shawl gave birth to a daughter, They Are Afraid of Her.

For a time, Crazy Horse was as content as he'd ever been. While he was never one for domestic life, he loved children and doted on They Are Afraid of Her. The happiness was not to last. In the spring of 1874, Crazy Horse returned from a raid against the Crow to discover that his lodge was black with mourning. His daughter had died, perhaps of cholera. The village had moved camp since her passing, and her death scaffold was some 70 miles away. Crazy Horse was distraught, and despite the large numbers of Crow war parties roaming through the area, he set off for the site. Two days later he found it. He climbed up on the scaffold and lay next to his daughter's body for three days and nights, letting neither food nor water pass his lips. His mourning complete, he returned to the Oglala.

CHAPTER FIVE

Fight for the Powder River Country

THE SUN SLIPPED BEHIND the Absaroka Range, and with it the surveyors called it a day. A crew of 20, all employed by the Northern Pacific Railroad, were charged with identifying the best route west through Dakota and Montana. The surveyors weren't alone. Under the command of Major Eugene M. Baker, a military escort of nearly 500 soldiers out of Fort Ellis accompanied them. It was the late summer of 1872, and building railroads was by then an enterprise that had the full support of the United States government, which was convinced of both the necessity and the inevitability of western expansion.

The survey crew made their way back across the Yellowstone River to their base camp opposite the mouth of Arrow Creek. They settled into another meal of pork and beans and began discussing the subject that was on all their minds.

"It's damn fine country out here."

"Yeah, it's grand, but is it safe?"

The surveyors knew they were in the heart of Teton Sioux country, but they had no inkling that the territory was so important to the Natives. The fertile plains rolling from the Yellowstone River (the Sioux knew it as the Elk River) teemed with animals. It had not always been Sioux territory. Not so long ago the Crow had called it home. Many Sioux died in the struggle to gain control of it, and they weren't about to let it slip through their fingers to the Wasichus.

"One of the officers was telling me that the Sioux aren't pleased to see us here. Said that a Sioux chief named Spotted Eagle met with Colonel Stanley in the spring. The chief said he knew that surveyors meant that a railroad was coming."

"Pretty sharp!"

The comment elicited an uneasy chuckle from the men.

"The Indian argued that his people had never agreed to allow a railroad through the territory south of the Yellowstone. Claimed the Laramie Treaty of '68 didn't allow it."

"Does it?"

"Hard to say. Could be argued that it's unceded territory. At least the Indians think it's theirs. Before Spotted Eagle left, he threatened that his people would tear up the railroad and kill its builders, until the last Sioux was dead."

"Damn." That seemed to sum it up, and the comment was met with silence.

Unbeknownst to the surveyors, the Sioux were aware of Baker's every move. They had known that the Wasichus were in the region long before they made camp at Arrow Creek. Early in the Moon of the Black Cherries (August), the bands had gathered along the Elk in southeastern Montana to celebrate a Sun Dance. There had been much talk about the Wasichus and their western movement. Once the celebrations were completed, Sioux leaders had met in council to decide how to deal with the intrusion. Crazy Horse was present, as was the Hunkpapa Sioux chief Sitting Bull.

Along with Red Cloud, Sitting Bull was one of two Teton Sioux with a reputation greater than Crazy Horse's at this time. Sitting Bull, however, had an advantage. Not only was he a great warrior, he was also a *wichasha wakan* (a holy man), to whom the future was revealed through visions. But Crazy Horse and Sitting Bull had

much in common. Their bands lived in the northern range of Teton
Sioux territory, where they had little contact with the Wasichus. Neither was anxious to make treaty that would open the area to the
newcomers. Indeed, both opposed Wasichus' travel and settlement
north of the Platte River, and they had raided in that region to
emphasize their position.

In 1867, a council of the Teton Sioux agreed to recognize Sitting
Bull as their supreme chief. The decision was a radical departure for
the Sioux. Never had they consented to fall in line behind one man.
There had been opposition to the proposal, but most who resisted
were persuaded to abandon their old mind-sets in the face of the new
threat posed by the Wasichus and their unsuccessful efforts to deal
with it. Others rejected such an appointment outright. Led by Spotted Tail and Red Cloud, the Brulé and the southern Oglala refused
to attend the council. Spotted Tail had chosen peace, and Red Cloud
was determined to wage his own war. Where exactly Crazy Horse fit
in is not clear. Reports suggest that the council appointed him Sitting Bull's second in command although Crazy Horse allied himself
with Red Cloud during the hostilities of 1867–68. Sitting Bull agreed
with Red Cloud's position during those bloody years, but he was not
actively engaged in the fighting along the Bozeman Trail. He also
refused to place his mark on the Fort Laramie Treaty of 1868.
Whether Crazy Horse and Sitting Bull had met at the great Sioux
council in 1867 or whether they had met at some previous time is
uncertain, but they were definitely in contact by the early 1870s.

The council called in the late summer of 1872 to discuss the
Wasichus' presence along the Elk was well attended by Hunkpapa,
Oglala, Sans Arc, Miniconjou, Blackfoot, a few Brulé and some
Cheyenne. The chiefs sat and listened as Sitting Bull addressed them.

"We've gathered to fight the Crow," he said, "but we have a much
greater problem. The Wasichus are above the Elk, where they have
no right to be. They are a grasping people, always wanting more.
We have allowed them to march along the Missouri. But now they
are at the banks of the Elk. Tomorrow they will be at the rivers that

One of a small number of images commonly suggested to be of Crazy Horse, allegedly taken at Fort Laramie in 1870. While some—including his Oglala contemporaries—maintain that Crazy Horse did have his picture taken, the evidence is against it. He was rarely seen at army forts before his surrender in the spring of 1877. Perhaps the picture was taken during the summer of 1877, but the photographer at the Red Cloud Agency left no record of it as would be expected given the importance of the subject. No one knows why Crazy Horse refused to have his picture taken, but it may have reflected a deep-seated childhood awkwardness about his appearance. The Native pictured above is without the facial scar that marked Crazy Horse and is dressed in costume he was not likely to wear.

flow through the Powder River country and perhaps even *Paha Sapa*."

They nodded heads and murmured agreement at this. All were aware that the land surrounding the Elk was as important to them as the blood that had been shed in taking it from the Crow.

"We have promised not to fight," continued Sitting Bull, his open hands before him, "but they have broken treaty. Those without honor will listen only to force," he said as he clenched his fists.

"It is soon time to hunt the buffalo. Perhaps our bullets are better used there," suggested one.

"If the white man comes, there will be no buffalo," countered Sitting Bull. "But my ears are open. It may be best to speak first with the Wasichus."

It was so agreed. The Moon of the Black Cherries (August) was full when 500 warriors rode to Arrow Creek. Was Sitting Bull prepared to talk with the Wasichus? Perhaps, but he was not given the opportunity. The Natives camped near Arrow Creek on August 13 and that night, young warriors anxious to prove their reputations slipped by the *akicita* and attacked the intruders.

Sitting Bull was wakened by the cracks of gunfire. He did not even have time to rise before a brave stood at the entrance to his lodge.

"Come," said Sitting Bull. "What has happened?"

"Young warriors, Brulés and Hunkpapa, have attacked the Wasichus' camp."

Sitting Bull smiled.

"The courage of youth. It seems our decision is made." There would be no parley with the Wasichus.

In the dark hours before sunrise, the warriors and the soldiers exchanged shots. As they settled into defensive positions to await the light of day, few casualties occurred. But one unfortunate Hunkpapa was Plenty Lice, who was shot as he rode the daring line, the open territory between opposing forces. Under a reddening sky, the Natives watched as the Wasichus threw his lifeless body on a campfire. They bristled at this act of disrespect.

Morning found Sitting Bull and Crazy Horse atop a bluff overlooking the battlefield.

"The Wasichus are well hidden," said Crazy Horse. "Our braves cannot reach them in the dense brush."

"Yes," agreed Sitting Bull. But he was less concerned with the position of the Wasichus than he was with the actions of the warriors.

"Our braves continue to run the daring line. There is no need for it. They have proven their courage. Look! It is the same group. They run for a third time!"

Crazy Horse squinted against the rising sun.

"They are not just any braves, Sitting Bull," he said recognizing them. "They are followers of Long Holy."

Sitting Bull sighed. Long Holy claimed to have had a vision, which he interpreted to mean that those who rode with him were cloaked by a magic, invisible blanket that prevented bullets from striking. Again and again, Long Holy rode his followers between the opposing forces. A few were hit, but none were killed as yet.

"It is enough," declared Sitting Bull. "Their courage has become foolishness. I cannot allow our young men to be wounded or to die. I will stop this."

Crazy Horse said nothing. He knew the importance of the daring line. He had ridden it himself earlier that morning. He was no Wasichu who went about barking orders at others, and he wasn't about to tell fighting warriors what they should or should not do. He remained on the bluff as Sitting Bull mounted his pony and rode down the gentle slope to the Sioux line. He could not hear what was said when Sitting Bull reached the warriors but Crazy Horse could see them shouting, and he suspected, using angry words. Surely Long Holy and his followers objected to Sitting Bull's interference.

What happened next took Crazy Horse by surprise.

Sitting Bull dismounted, took his pipe and tobacco from a pouch on his pony, and with his weapons in hand, walked to the open land stretching between the opposing forces. There he sat, the two eagle feathers in his hair identifying him as a simple Sioux warrior, little different than his brothers. Crazy Horse saw him wave to the warriors, a signal that they join him. It was a challenge as much as an invitation. Soon four others joined him. The two Sioux and two Cheyenne took their journey on shaky legs. When they arrived, Crazy Horse watched Sitting Bull as he calmly filled the bowl of his pipe, and with flint and steel, lit it. Placing the stem between his lips, he contentedly took a few long, deep drags. He passed the pipe to his companions, whose trembling hands and short quick puffs suggested they were more aware than was Sitting Bull of the small clouds of earth kicked up around them by the enemies' bullets. The pipe made a few rounds before the ball of tobacco was spent.

Once it was, Crazy Horse watched Sitting Bull pick up a stick and clean out the bowl. He placed it back in his pouch, rose and walked slowly back to the admiring Sioux line, his limp emphasized for effect. He hadn't taken many steps when the others rushed past him, impeded neither by courage nor disability. Crazy Horse noticed that one left in such haste that he forgot his weapons. He chuckled when the man chose not to retrieve them.

When Sitting Bull arrived back at the Sioux line, he was greeted with silent awe. Who had ever seen such an act of bravery? Was there a coup counted that displayed such courage? What words could give recognition to his daring? To a people who placed great value in a man's willingness to risk his own life in the face of great danger, Sitting Bull's action was unmatched. Even Crazy Horse was impressed. He could not let such an act go unanswered. He charged his pony down the slope and rode the daring line himself. His pony was killed, but Crazy Horse made it back to the Sioux line uninjured. It was a courageous act, but everyone knew that it did not match what Sitting Bull had done.

When Crazy Horse returned to the warriors, Sitting Bull broke the silence.

"It is enough. Today's fighting is over."

None questioned his decision. With their morale intact, the warriors pulled back. The Battle of Arrow Creek was indecisive; neither side could claim a clear victory. But the fighting had deepened the surveyors' fears. They refused to go south of the Yellowstone and made hurried measurements near the northerly Musselshell River before hastily retreating to Fort Ellis. Spotted Eagle's prediction hadn't quite been met, but the Sioux could claim, with some truth, that their first blow against the Northern Pacific Railroad, and everything it stood for, was a successful one.

Success, however, was short lived. The episode and others like it elsewhere on the Plains only strengthened American resolve. William Tecumseh Sherman, general-in-chief of the army, voiced that determination before Congress in early 1873.

"The Northern Pacific Railroad is a national enterprise. We are forced to protect those who survey and construct it from the most warlike Indians on the continent. They will fight for every foot of the line." Left unspoken, of course, was the American willingness to engage them in that battle, regardless of where the line—or the death count—might go.

Crazy Horse wasn't involved with the Wasichus in the months following the Battle at Arrow Creek. He was busy hunting buffalo and raiding the Crow. Sioux warriors enjoyed great victories against their traditional enemies in 1873. Perhaps Crazy Horse even agreed with Sitting Bull, who declared after the fight at Arrow Creek that he would no longer fight the Wasichus unless they brought the battle to the Sioux.

Sitting Bull did fight again because the soldiers and surveyors continued to come. And in the late summer of 1873, the Sioux and the army met near where the Bighorn River joined with the Yellowstone River. It is possible that Crazy Horse fought alongside Sitting Bull in this battle. Again the fighting proved inconclusive, with few losses on either side. But the Battle of the Yellowstone was an important one. The series of skirmishes with the Sioux supported Sherman's prediction, and eastern financiers were reluctant to fund western railroad expansion in the face of huge costs. For the time being, the steel would not roll past Bismarck, in the northern center of Dakota.

William Tecumseh Sherman (1820–91) in the 1860s; Commander
of the Division of the Missouri, then the army's general-in-chief

   The Battle of the Yellowstone also introduced the Sioux to a
Wasichu who was to be instrumental to their future: Lieutenant
Colonel George Armstrong Custer, who they came to know as Long
Hair. Along with the Seventh Cavalry, Custer was ordered into the

upper Missouri River region to provide support for the little rail-road construction that continued.

～～～

As the spring of 1874 came to the Missouri River, Fort Abraham Lincoln was at the mercy of the heat and the mosquitoes. It was damn uncomfortable. Only the recent order from General Sheridan that the men would be moving south to explore the Black Hills brought any hope of relief. But the departure date was still weeks away, and Custer, charged with leading the expedition, was irritated. The bugs and the weather were bearable, but somehow the Natives had discovered the army's plan, and the continuous stream of Sioux intent on dissuading his Seventh Calvary from their exploratory mission was trying his patience. He bit his tongue and listened to yet another one.

"The Black Hills are *Paha Sapa*, they are sacred," explained the Sioux. "They are our home. They have been since the beginning."

"The beginning doesn't matter anymore, chief," sighed Custer. "Fact is that times have changed. Plenty of mystery surrounds those hills, and Americans want to know what's in them."

"But the Laramie Treaty places *Paha Sapa* in the Great Sioux Reservation," objected the Sioux.

"Well, now, if you'd read that treaty, you'd know that the American government can send its officials onto that reservation whenever it wants. Sorry chief, there's nothing you can do about it. Good day." Custer looked down at some papers on his desk, ending the conversation and dismissing the visitor. He made a mental note to tell his assistant that he wouldn't speak to any more Natives regardless of how important they appeared.

The Blacks Hills Expedition set out on July 2, 1874, marching south to the regimental band's rendition of *The Girl I Left Behind Me*. At the front of the column on his favorite bay horse was Custer. He cut a dashing figure, his long reddish blond hair falling to his shoulders beneath a slouch hat pinned up on the left side. A generous and

General George Armstrong Custer (1839–76) in the 1860s; Commander of the Seventh Cavalry; leader of the Black Hills Expedition

unkempt moustache gave little hint of a mouth. Fringes hung from
the arms of his buckskin jacket and lustrous black riding boots
reached up to his knees. A pistol butt extended from his belt and the
tip of his long sword fell beneath his heel. Here was the kind of
adventure he wanted, and he was ready.

Flamboyant, courageous and enthusiastic, Custer had attracted attention since his days at West Point some 15 years earlier. While he hadn't been a stellar cadet, superiors took note of his potential during the Civil War. After the War Between the States, Custer accepted a posting on the Plains, certain that the glory he sought would be found in the subjugation of the Natives. However, he was forced to postpone his plans when, in late 1867, he was given a year's suspension for disobeying orders. Fortunately for Custer, army brass brought General Philip Sheridan into the Department of the Missouri with orders to rein in hostile Natives. Sheridan wanted men whose desire to fight was unquestioned, and he remembered Custer, who had caught the general's eye during the Civil War. Sheridan applied for Custer's reinstatement, and in the fall of 1868, Custer joined the general at Camp Supply on the Beaver Creek.

Custer was anxious to polish his tarnished reputation and knew he had an opportunity to do so when Sheridan gave him command of the Seventh Cavalry. Custer and his troops were ordered south to the Washita River, where they enjoyed a crushing victory over Black Kettle's Cheyenne in November 1868. The years that followed Custer's triumph at the Washita saw no other events quite so dramatic. Eventually, he was transferred to Fort Rice and ordered to protect the surveying crews of the Northern Pacific Railroad. Throughout 1873, the Sioux nipped at his flanks with frustrating regularity although injury and theft were never more than minimal. Still, combined with other Sioux efforts on the Yellowstone River, it was enough to stall plans for the railroad's western expansion. The Sioux raids also had an unforeseen result. The raids gave the army an excuse to reconnoiter in the Black Hills, a mysterious mountain region that was subject to tantalizing rumors of gold.

The Black Hills Expedition consisted of 10 companies of the Seventh Cavalry along with additional teamsters and civilians (reporters, miners and scientists), for a total of about 1000. In late July, the Seventh Cavalry reached the outskirts of the Black Hills, a name that does disservice to both their size and rich colors. Even

General Philip Sheridan (1831–88) in the 1860s; led the campaign against the Natives for the Department of the Missouri

a cursory glance at the land that rolled to the base of the hills was enough to convince Custer that it was suited for grazing. The many stands of oak and poplar provided ready building material and fuel. Peaks towered over hidden valleys, and before their majesty, even a pragmatic military man like Custer stood in awe. They cradled blue lakes of clear, alkali-free water and fresh streams that fed the Cheyenne River. Colorful flowers bloomed on the shorelines, across open grasslands and up the hillsides. Everything about the Black Hills suggested that they were suited to agriculture. Animals were also plentiful, and Custer could easily appreciate why the Sioux held the area so dear.

As he described these details in his official report, he knew it would be difficult to block the arrival of settlers, who would surely want access to the uncommonly inspiring region. When he included the expedition's discovery of gold, he knew that it would be impossible.

Custer was right. Despite his words of caution, "Until further examination is made regarding the richness of gold, no opinion about its quantity should be formed," the discovery took on a life of its own. Reporters bore the initial responsibility for America's enthusiasm.

Some, like Samuel Barrows of the *New York Tribune,* counseled due care. He wrote ominously, "Those who seek the Hills only for gold must be prepared to take their chances....The Black Hills...are not without ready-made monuments for the martyrs who may perish in their peaks."

But such advice was mostly lost in the enthusiastic and exaggerated stories more commonly written by journalists. Newspapers and magazines from across the nation reprinted the intoxicating observations of William Eleroy Curtis of the *Chicago Inter-Ocean,* who declared that the Black Hills held great promise, assuring all, "From the grassroots down it was pay dirt."

Soon wide-eyed readers were babbling about the New Eldorado. As profit-minded entrepreneurs in the towns of Cheyenne, Bismarck and Sioux City massaged reports, folks were led to believe that easy fortune awaited. Gold fever boiled in men's blood, and within a year, over 1000 prospectors were toiling in the Black Hills. More were en route along what the Sioux called "Thieves Road," the trail that Custer took on his expedition.

The army took the position that the miners shouldn't be there. That position was in line with the United States' treaty obligation to the Sioux, which not only gave the Natives title to the Black Hills, but also assured them that United States officials were the only people permitted there. But the army's policy was based more on practical concerns than legal or ethical ones. It didn't want to cause trouble with the formidable Sioux. The army prevented some prospectors from arriving, and it expelled others. Despite its desire and efforts, neither of which could be described as zealous, prospectors kept coming. Soon, prospectors, promoters and ordinary citizens were exerting irresistible pressure on the federal government. The message was clear: do what had to be done, but get control of the Black Hills.

To address the troubling situation, the Allison Commission was established and charged with extinguishing Native title to the region. In September 1875, the commissioners arrived at the Red Cloud Agency, just south of the Great Sioux Reservation near Camp Robinson. They sent word to the agency Natives (those who had made treaty with the United States government and lived on the reservation) that they wished to discuss terms for purchasing the Black Hills. The assumption was that agency Natives would be more willing to deal than the more independent hunting bands would be.

The Sioux who had opposed treaty were also approached to determine their opinion on the Allison Commission's terms. It was necessary to send someone into the Powder River country to talk with Crazy Horse and Sitting Bull because they would not travel south to the Red Cloud Agency to discuss such a matter. Under ordinary circumstances, a single runner might have visited the resisting bands to relay terms and return with replies. However, the mission was too important. The Wasichus were serious about buying *Paha Sapa*, and the message had to be delivered to two of the most powerful and respected Sioux leaders.

At the direction of the local Indian agent, Young Man Afraid of His Horses, an Oglala chief and head of the Red Cloud Agency police, left his reservation on the White River in late summer and led a small delegation of Natives north into the Powder River country. He was joined by Frank Grouard, a mixed-blood (White and either Polynesian or Black) interpreter who had lived with the Oglala for some years and was well known to them. They took many packhorses heavy with trade goods to be given as gifts. Young Man Afraid hoped that the gifts might encourage Crazy Horse and Sitting Bull to consider the Wasichus' offer, but even as he rode, he knew that they were not likely to be receptive.

The emissaries first reached the Tongue River, where they discovered 2000 lodges, mostly Sioux and Cheyenne, all followers of Crazy Horse. They were of one mind when it came to the Wasichus: the newcomers had no right to be in the Powder River country, and if they ventured there, they would feel the blow of the war club. The villagers guessed the mission of Young Man Afraid and his companions, and for a time, it seemed that they would drive the emissaries from the camp. Cooler heads prevailed, however, and Young Man Afraid was able to make his way to the chief's tipi.

"Crazy Horse, my old friend, will you come south to discuss *Paha Sapa*?" asked Young Man Afraid. "It is important that the voice of all Sioux be heard."

"I have nothing to say," replied Crazy Horse. "My arrows, my bullets speak for me."

"And they have spoken well. But it is time for words. You know that I do not wish to sell *Paha Sapa*. But I do not think that it can be kept by going on the warpath. If we speak to the Great Father as one, perhaps he will respect our wishes."

"Ha!" laughed Crazy Horse. "The Wasichus have shown what they think of our wishes. The Sioux no longer speak as one. Red Cloud and his Hang-Around-The-Fort people have become dependent on what the Great Father gives them. They want to sell *Paha Sapa* to keep their master happy," he growled.

"They have made treaty and they do not want. It is more than can be said for your followers," suggested Young Man Afraid, who had seen the near-empty parfleches and had guessed that the hunt had not been successful. "Your influence is best used to provide for your followers."

"I will provide for them in my own way, as the Sioux have always done, as Wakan Tanka wishes," continued Crazy Horse. "What influence I have will be used to keep the Wasichus far from us and off the land that our fathers died upon. I will not be convinced that *Paha Sapa* should be sold to the Wasichus."

Crazy Horse bent over and took a pinch of dirt from the ground.

"I will not sell, not even as much as this," he said, as he let the dirt fall from his fingers. "One does not sell the earth upon which the people walk.

"Still," added Crazy Horse, "I am no Wasichu, and those who want to make treaty can go."

Young Man Afraid left without the Crazy Horse's support, but the Oglala chief joined him and Grouard when they traveled to the camp of the Hunkpapa chief Sitting Bull the next day.

"*Paha Sapa* is our food basket. It is there for us in times of need. As long as there is game, I will never come in," replied Sitting Bull.

The Hunkpapa chief nodded in agreement when Big Breast added, "All those that are in favor of selling land from their children, let them go."

Few Sioux took up the offer of Crazy Horse and Sitting Bull to make treaty. Indeed, most were incensed by the treaty offer, and some made plans to kill the messengers. When Crazy Horse got wind of the proposed attack, he met with the leaders, called them all by name and told them that they must keep their knives sheathed. Young Man Afraid and the others could not be killed because they delivered a message.

"My friends," added Crazy Horse, "whoever tries to murder these people will have to fight me, too."

Crazy Horse's reputation was such that all talk of attack ended. The next day Young Man Afraid, Grouard and their party returned to the Red Cloud Agency without the support of either of the two

Sioux leaders who were most firmly opposed to the sale of the Black Hills. But, as predicted by government officials, the agency Natives and some of the northern Natives who were tired of fighting were willing to listen. These Natives met with the Allison Commission in late September 1875. The council was tense, however, because thousands of Natives opposed to the treaty camped near thousands more Natives who wished to negotiate. Rebellious songs and gunfire designed to intimidate those who wished to negotiate emphasized heartfelt opposition to the discussions.

The participants had not yet settled in when Little Big Man, who had been sent south by Crazy Horse to watch over the proceedings, burst into the treaty circle. He held a rifle high above the single eagle feather on his headband. He wore only a breechcloth and he was painted for war, but most were looking at the wounds on his chest, still freshly scarred from the ritual sacrifice of the Sun Dance.

"I will kill the first chief who speaks for selling *Paha Sapa*!" he shouted. "Go to your lodges my foolish young friends. Go to your lodges, and do not return until your heads have cooled," he advised.

They went, but some chiefs would not be bullied by the likes of Little Big Man. One of them was Red Cloud. He disagreed with both Crazy Horse's and Sitting Bull's leadership as well as their pro-war attitude. And while he had previously touched the pen, his words in council showed that he still retained his old fighting spirit.

"Surely you are aware that Americans are in the Black Hills," said one of the commissioners after the council had reconvened. "That is not likely to change. More will certainly move into the unceded territory—the Powder River country. We are presenting you with an opportunity, one that will see you justly compensated for the territory. The offer is $6 million dollars."

"The Laramie Treaty says that *Paha Sapa* are ours forever," replied Red Cloud. "My people fought for that, and it is only fitting because they have always been ours. But I am a realistic man, and although the changes that come are difficult to accept, accept them I will. For $70 million dollars."

"Seventy million!" exclaimed the commissioners in concert.

"That is hardly reasonable," barked one.

"Reasonable or not, it is my price," concluded Red Cloud.

His demand ended the council. The commissioners returned to Washington, angry and frustrated. In their final report, they suggested that the government fix a "fair" price for the Black Hills and present the offer to the Sioux as a *fait accompli*. Then they left the matter to the politicians.

≈≈≈

In late 1875, President Ulysses Grant met with his most senior officials to discuss the dilemma of Black Hills. It was a meeting that Grant had hoped to avoid, but the Allison Commission had failed, leaving the government in a most difficult position. Settlers were pressing for access to the region, and there seemed no certain way to keep them out. Yet, the government had given its word to the Sioux that the Black Hills would remain Native territory. While the participants had some differences at the meeting, they quickly settled on a plan of action that recognized the new order in the West.

"It seems, gentlemen," concluded the president, placing his hands on the table as he rose above those seated around him, "that the only solution is war."

"It is justified," agreed Secretary of War William Belknap. "The Sioux have been raiding the territory around the Yellowstone River for some time, clearly in violation of the '68 Laramie Treaty."

"But," said General George Crook, "those Sioux did not sign the treaty."

"Goddammit, George! A Sioux is a Sioux," bellowed General William Sherman. "The president is right. The Indians will not succumb until they feel the full military might of the United States."

"It's settled then," said Grant. "The order barring miners from the Black Hills will remain in effect, but we will make no effort to enforce it. The miners' presence will soon put an end to the dispute over possession. We will also demand that all Sioux hunting bands return to the agencies. Once there, they can be made dependent on annuities and trade goods. A dependent people is a compliant people."

"And the teeth of the order, sir?" asked Secretary of the Interior Zachariah Chandler. "What will we do if the bands refuse to return? The hostility of Crazy Horse and Sitting Bull towards American settlers is well known, and it is unlikely they will obey the order."

"You will direct the commissioner of Indian Affairs to notify all Sioux and Cheyenne living off the reservation to go to the reservation before January 31. Should they fail to do so, they will be considered hostile Indians, enemies of the American government. The army will be charged with ensuring that all hostiles obey."

When February arrived, neither Crazy Horse nor Sitting Bull had come in to the Great Sioux Reservation. They were labeled hostile, and within days, the government declared war on them and the other Sioux who failed to obey the government's order.

It was difficult for the northern Sioux to do as the government wished because most of them were not aware of the government's order. The Moon of the Dark Red Calves (February) came and went, and the northern Sioux had no idea that they had suddenly become hostiles and enemies of the United States. For the most part, late 1875 and early 1876 saw Crazy Horse and the members of the other bands living much as they always had. They hunted, traded and occasionally raided the Crow. But the Wasichus were never far from their thoughts, and so to remind the newcomers of the northern Natives' continuing displeasure with their presence, early in the year, some Sioux and Cheyenne forced the evacuation of Fort Pease, near Bozeman.

By the Moon of the Snowblind (March), most of the bands, including Crazy Horse's, were informed by runners that the government considered them hostile and that they would be attacked unless they came into an agency. The Oglala held a council to discuss the news. Some expressed concern that there might be an attack while the snow was still on the ground. If that happened, the women and children would suffer terribly. Crazy Horse's own wife, Black Shawl, was ill with tuberculosis, so he might have shared this concern. But when he addressed the council, it was clear that he had more than the health of individual Sioux on his mind.

"No man can fight when the hearts of his women have fallen down," he conceded. "But for me, there is no country that can hold the tracks of the moccasin and the boots of the Wasichu side by side."

Eventually, most agreed that it was more important to hunt buffalo and fill the parfleches than it was to meet the demands of the Wasichus. Those who wanted to go to the agency could do so. Perhaps others might consider following them next spring.

However, everything changed before then.

On March 17, 1876, the army showed that it was serious about carrying out the government's new policy. Just before dawn, six cavalry troops attacked Two Moons' camp along the Powder River just north of the Wyoming border. Mostly Cheyenne and a few Sioux populated the camp. Some accounts describe them as peaceful Natives who had decided to go to the Red Cloud Agency rather than fight while others suggest they were on the way to join forces with Crazy Horse. He Dog and the Cheyenne medicine man Ice, both good friends of Crazy Horse, were in Two Moons' camp, so it seems they were making for Crazy Horse's camp although Two Moons later denied it.

Frank Grouard was the army's lead scout on the cavalry expedition. He led the soldiers to the camp by mistake. Grouard thought it was Crazy Horse's band, possibly because he recognized He Dog, who often rode with Crazy Horse. Grouard was pleased with the discovery. He had harbored a grudge against Crazy Horse ever since the failed effort to convince the chief to accept treaty in the summer of 1875. That mission had been important to Grouard, who was anxious to ingratiate himself with his army superiors. Crazy Horse's rejection had been embarrassing. But here was an opportunity for revenge.

As the army approached the camp, Grouard shouted, "Crazy Horse! You told me you would rather fight than make treaty. Now is the time to come out and get the fighting you want. The troops surround your camp!"

The only responses were the startled cries of the awakening camp. The cavalry quickly charged but it had lost the element of surprise because of Grouard. It was a poorly planned and commanded assault, and the Cheyenne were able to hold their own for awhile. Eventually, however, they were forced to abandon their camp, which the Wasichus burned to the ground. At the mercy of winter's icy grip (it was between –40° and –50° Fahrenheit), the refugee Cheyenne stumbled into Crazy Horse's camp at nearby Pumpkin Creek. On their arrival, the two chiefs met, and Two Moons described the incident.

"We were not looking for a fight, but the Wasichus have brought the battle to us," proclaimed Two Moons. "Crazy Horse's stand against the Wasichu invaders is well known. Now the Cheyenne stand with you."

"We welcome you with open arms. Let us go and see Sitting Bull," said Crazy Horse.

When the Oglala and Cheyenne arrived at the Hunkpapa camp, they were greeted enthusiastically. The arrivals marveled at the generosity of the Hunkpapa, who opened their parfleches and resupplied them. The mood turned black, however, when Two Moons told Sitting Bull of the unprovoked attack. The chief was incensed.

"Who are these Wasichus?" he shouted. "They agree that *Paha Sapa* is ours forever and then they demand to own it. They will give us money for food. I get my food from *Paha Sapa* and do not need what the Wasichus offer. It is known that I accept no price for them. And when they learn of this? They attack! They are not to be trusted."

"My brothers," he continued, more reserved but still intense, "we are as islands in a lake of Wasichus. If we continue to stand separately, they will destroy us all. We must unite. For many moons I have raised my lance only in self-defense. I have been patient and put up with much. Well, now the Wasichus have come shooting. They have brought war. War they will have."

Sitting Bull, with the support of Crazy Horse who recognized the Hunkpapa chief's leadership, dispatched runners to every Sioux, Cheyenne and Arapaho camp west of the Missouri River. He asked them to join with him and engage the Wasichus in one great battle along the Rosebud Creek. Many responded to his call, and spring 1876 saw the trails that led to his camp thick with Natives. The sight was a testament to the respect Sitting Bull commanded and to their desperation. Although not everyone who heard his plea came, soon nearly 500 lodges were gathered, representing more than 1000 warriors. Among them was Crazy Horse and his band.

In late spring, Sitting Bull called a war council. The council selected him to lead the Sioux attack, while Two Moons would command the Cheyenne. By early June, the uncommonly large gathering of Natives, united by a single, monumental cause, made their way towards Rosebud Creek, just east of the Little Bighorn River. More Natives arrived daily, and by the Moon When the Ponies Shed (May), 4000 warriors were camped near the Rosebud Creek preparing for battle. Government officials were aware of the movement, and they suspected that something was up. Indian agents were especially concerned. In the years after the signing of the 1868 Laramie Treaty, a steady stream of Natives had come into the agencies. Suddenly, only old men, women, children and precious few warriors populated the agencies. Most of the warriors had ridden north.

Sitting Bull walked through the camps and sang his new war song:

You tribes, what are you saying?
I have been a war chief.
All the same, I'm still living.

Warriors listened and nodded in silent agreement.

The Moon of Making Fat (June) was only a sliver when the annual Sun Dance commenced. The ceremony honored Wi, the sun, the great spirit that reigned over the world of the living and the dead. The celebration was lengthy, lasting 12 days, during which the tribes performed ritualized ceremonies that reinforced the tribal ideals and mores. The greater part of the Sun Dance, however, was devoted to the preparation of the dancers and to the dance itself. Those who participated subjected themselves to self-torture in the belief that such sacrifice would be looked upon favorably by Wakan Tanka.

Warriors endured stages of self-torture, usually including dancing to exhaustion, the ritualized cutting of arms, and finally, the skewering of the flesh of the chest and the back. The men hung from the skewers until they ripped through muscle and flesh. The culmination of the Sun Dance was a communal dance. When the band completed this ritual, its shared sense of identity was reinforced. Sitting Bull knew that it was just what the Sioux and their allies needed on this occasion.

Undoubtedly Crazy Horse realized this as well but, as usual, he was not in camp for the ceremony. He had his own ways of preparing for battles, and they did not involve others. Perhaps he reflected on his vision or sought to communicate with spirits for guidance. He returned to camp when the Sun Dance was complete, carrying a brown calfskin cape dotted with white spots reminiscent of the hailstorm in his vision. He returned to good news.

Sitting Bull had endured a most painful sacrifice. With a sharp awl, his brother Jumping Bull removed 50 pieces of flesh each about the size of a match head from both arms. The blood flowed freely until Wakan Tanka had a red blanket, which was a necessary part of the ritual. Sitting Bull had then danced barefoot on gravel for most of one day. Finally, Wakan Tanka granted him a vision. Crazy Horse heard it from Black Moon, the Hunkpapa *wichasha wakan* to whom Sitting Bull had whispered it before he collapsed.

"He told me to tell everyone that he'd heard a voice commanding him to look below the sun," explained Black Moon. "As he did, he saw many soldiers falling to the ground in our camp, their heads below their feet. Under them were some Natives, also upside down. Again, the voice spoke to him, 'These Wasichus do not have ears. They will die, but do not take their belongings.' "

"The vision reveals that the Wasichus will not leave us in peace, that they will attack us and we will win," added Back Moon.

But Crazy Horse had stopped listening once Sitting Bull's vision had been described. He did not need it explained.

"Shadows grow long and old ways disappear in the dark. Yet, warriors may take heart," said Crazy Horse.

Black Moon gave Crazy Horse a puzzled look as the great warrior walked away.

A few days later, the Natives broke camp. They didn't go far. By the middle of June, they were heading for the valley of the Greasy Grass, where they saw good signs of buffalo. They had many to feed, and seeing the sign was a good omen, another blessing from Wakan Tanka. While most traveled west following the animals' tracks, the Cheyenne sent out a small scouting party. The leader, Little Hawk, brought down a buffalo, and while they were roasting it, one pointed to a nearby hill.

"Look! Up there. Two braves," he said.

"Must be Sioux scouts," suggested Little Hawk. "Let's play a trick on them. We'll sneak around the hill and come up behind them. We'll see how good these Sioux really are!"

Little Hawk led the Cheyenne to a gully that approached the hill. They followed it, climbing out when they found an easy trail to the summit.

"If their skills are such that we can sneak up on them, be careful. They might not know we are Cheyenne," laughed Little Hawk.

When they reached the top of the hill, the scouts were gone. Little Hawk gazed to the plains that spread out towards the Rosebud Creek on the far side of the hill and slipped immediately from his horse.

"Get down," he hissed, waving his hand to urge the others to do so.

"It's only two Sioux scouts," replied one of the braves. "No need to be so cautious."

"They were not Sioux scouts," said Little Hawk. "Rees or Crow, perhaps. Only they scout for the Wasichus."

"What?"

"The plains are black with Wasichus!" cried Little Hawk. "I have never seen so many. Quick, let us return to camp."

It was not long before they were there. Little Hawk rode his pony through the camp, shouting "Get all the young men ready and let us set out. A fight awaits on the Rosebud."

~~~~~~

By the spring of 1876, the army was moving on President Grant's order to rein in the hostile Sioux. General Philip Sheridan, still commander of the Department of the Missouri, was charged with organizing the campaign. Sheridan had been at the forefront of the United States' battle with the Plains Natives for more than a decade. Following distinguished service in the Civil War, he was posted to the Plains. Perhaps authorities appreciated his attitude as much as his ability.

Around the time of his new posting, Sheridan declared, "The only good Indian is a dead Indian." In 1874 he had been a driving force behind the defeat of the southern Plains Natives, and he was expected to achieve similar results in the north.

Sheridan gave General Alfred Terry command of the offensive against the northern Sioux. Sheridan had no doubt about where Terry's sympathies lay. He was one of the commissioners who had agreed to close the Bozeman Trail back in 1868. He did not forget easily. Red Cloud's War was a defeat that still rankled, as did the failure of the Allison Commission on which Terry had served as a member.

Terry mustered the largest force ever to ride against the Sioux. General George Crook and 1200 troops marched northwest from Fort Fetterman along the eastern slopes of the Bighorn Mountains. General John Gibbon and 450 troops marched east from Fort Ellis along the Yellowstone River. George Armstrong Custer and 1000 troops marched west from Fort Abraham Lincoln, following the Yellowstone River to the mouth of the Powder River. Terry, who had no experience fighting on the Plains, rode with Custer. The plan was for the three columns to converge on the Sioux in the Powder River

General Alfred Terry (1827–90) in the 1860s. He signed the 1868
Fort Laramie Treaty and served on the 1875 Allison Commission.

country. But, while the army was still searching for the Sioux, the
Natives discovered Crook (whom they called Three Stars because
of his insignia of rank) and his men on the Rosebud Creek.

When the Cheyenne scouts returned to the camp, Crazy Horse quickly organized the warriors. Sitting Bull's role was limited in this affair because he remained weak from his Sun Dance activities. Crazy Horse directed 1500 warriors to remain in the camp to protect the women, children and elderly. Another 1500 were to ride with him against Crook. Undoubtedly, it was difficult for many of the warriors to accept their assignment as camp guards. The Sun Dance, the accompanying ceremonies and celebrations and Sitting Bull's vision were so inspirational that no one wanted to stay in camp where they could anticipate little action or honor. On June 16, 1876 ,the 1500 warriors rode out. Crazy Horse, ever mindful of the impulsiveness of young warriors, gave strict orders to the *akicita* to ensure none broke from the war party. He didn't want Three Stars to have even the slightest inkling that warriors were approaching.

Stopping only long enough for the warriors to make their battle preparations, Crazy Horse arrived at the valley of the Rosebud Creek on the morning of June 17. Joined by some scouts, he climbed a hill that overlooked the valley for a quick reconnaissance. To the east, the Wasichus were camped along the river. Crazy Horse observed the surroundings. The river split the mile-wide valley, which was mostly uneven terrain. It would not be an easy place to fight. The valley narrowed to the north, forming a canyon. Crazy Horse thought that the location was a promising place for an ambush.

"Crow!" called one of the scouts. "They've seen us!"

The army's Native scouts were busy. For days they had sensed the Sioux were near, and they had told Crook as much. The general had ordered them to watch carefully. He didn't know if their information was reliable but, as an experienced Native fighter who had enjoyed success forcing Natives onto reservations on the southern Plains, he knew that scouts in the field couldn't hurt. He watched as the Crow scouts scampered down the bluff to the west. Crook could see that they were shouting, but he couldn't make out their words.

General George Crook (1828–90). General William T. Sherman
considered Crook to be the army's greatest Native fighter ever.
The honor was earned after a lifetime of engagements through the
western and southern United States. He had fought the Yakama in
the Columbia region, the Paiute in Idaho Territory and the Apache
in Arizona before he was given command of the Department of
the Platte and ordered to rein in the Plains Natives. His one major
encounter with Crazy Horse was the Battle of the Rosebud in June
1876. Crook claimed victory, but his assertion was shared by few.
Most agreed that Crazy Horse had won the day. The Sioux called
Crook "Three Stars" because of the three stars he wore on his
uniform. He was, in fact, a one-star general.

Soon words were unnecessary. Within moments, the Sioux swept around the base of the hill.

Once the Sioux and Cheyenne warriors were aware that the army's Native scouts had seen them, the best efforts of the *akicita* could not keep them in line. Crazy Horse signaled to them to let the warriors go because the element of surprise had been lost. Indeed, Crazy Horse realized quickly that the soundest strategy was to strike fast before the Wasichus could organize a defense. The warriors might have rolled through the camp had the 250 Crow and Shoshone warriors allied with the army not fought so bravely. Their determination gave the soldiers valuable time to prepare.

Crook barked orders for a counterattack, and under pressure from the advancing soldiers, the Sioux fell back.

Short Bull, a Sioux who participated in the fight, described what happened: "Crazy Horse, Bad Heart Bull, Black Deer, Kicking Bear and Good Weasel turned the charge and got the soldiers on the run....When these five commenced to rally their men, that was as far as the soldiers got."

The success that Crazy Horse and his companions enjoyed in halting the Wasichus' advance had more to do with strategy than with numbers. Given the desire of the warriors to fight independently, only a small number of the total Native force joined his charge. But those who did followed Crazy Horse's example and fought in a different way. Rather than lay back and exchange distant fire as was the usual with the Wasichus, they exploded into the fray, fighting hand-to-hand in the manner of traditional Native warfare.

Colonel Anson Mills described the Sioux "charging boldly and rapidly through the soldiers, knocking them from their horses with lances and knives, dismounting and killing them, cutting off the arms of some at the elbows in the middle of the fight and carrying them off."

Crook then made a series of decisions that almost resulted in the decimation of his command. He believed that Crazy Horse's camp was downstream, and he dispatched Mills and eight troops of cavalry to find and capture it. Then, worried about the warriors' effectiveness in pinning his men down, he divided the rest of his command into two groups, hoping that one might offer support to the other.

Crazy Horse must have smiled as he watched the Wasichus carry out their orders. Mills' men marched towards the canyon. Crazy Horse directed warriors there to wait in ambush. He ordered others to fall behind Crook's two newly formed groups and attack the weak points along the flanks and from the rear. When scouts informed Crook that the troops were being surrounded and that there was imminent danger that they might be separated, he sent a hurried message to Mills to return. Mills pulled back with some relief. He had seen the canyon and was none too certain about venturing through it. Doubling back, Mills' men approached the warriors from the rear. The warriors weren't expecting the maneuver, and they broke off the attack. Crook's men were tired from the marching and fighting, so he did not order them to pursue.

The Battle of the Rosebud seemed to be a draw. Losses were similar—28 soldiers died and 56 were wounded, while 36 Natives died and 63 were wounded. Both sides, however, claimed victory. Crook's confident assessment was based on the fact that the Sioux and Cheyenne were the first to retreat. Those who fought with Crazy Horse believed that he used good judgment in the battle.

Black Elk asserted, "Crazy Horse whipped Three Stars on the Rosebud that day, and I think he could have rubbed the soldiers out there. He could have called many more warriors from the villages and he could have rubbed the soldiers out...."

Perhaps Black Elk was right, but the real measure of Crazy Horse's victory was that he neutralized Three Stars, who then retreated south to his camp at Goose Creek, where he remained for the next eight weeks, oblivious to subsequent events to the north along the Little Bighorn River. It was strange behavior for one with his enviable reputation for fighting Natives.

A fanciful engraving of the Sioux attack on General Crook's men at the Battle of the Rosebud, published in August 1876

For their part, the Sioux and Cheyenne packed up their camp and moved to the valley of the Greasy Grass (Little Bighorn River) in their ongoing search for buffalo. Warriors rode with their weapons close at hand. Everyone knew that there would be more fighting because Sitting Bull's vision had revealed that the Wasichus would attack the Native camp, which had not happened on the Rosebud. But they were not afraid. They had handled Three Stars, and Sitting Bull's vision inspired confidence. A week after the Battle of the Rosebud, they made camp in a wooded valley south of the fork of the Bighorn and Little Bighorn rivers.

Meanwhile, Generals Gibbon, Terry and Custer and their troops had arrived at the mouth of the Rosebud Creek. Scouts reported that many Sioux tracks led towards the Little Bighorn River, and they declared that a Sioux camp was in the region. The generals decided to divide their troops and move on the camp. Custer marched his men south along the west bank of the Rosebud. Gibbon's troops also headed south, but they took the east bank of the Little Bighorn. Terry's troops took up the rear. They believed that Crook was still approaching the Rosebud from the south. The goal was to surround the hostiles and cut off any escape. Strategically, the plan was sound enough, but in Custer's eyes, it was riddled with shortcomings, not the least of which was the timing. The attack was set for the morning of June 26, and Custer was concerned that the hostiles might well be gone by then. He was thinking about the problem when his assistant interrupted him.

"Sir, the Ree scouts are here as you requested."

"Send them in."

As the two Ree stood before him, Custer revealed his deepest desire.

"You're aware that we will soon commence our attack on the Sioux and Cheyenne. It is an important battle, and I am counting on your assistance. When we defeat the hostiles, I will soon be the Great Father," confided Custer, "and your people will be rewarded."

Custer was only too aware of the American tradition of elevating its war heroes to the presidency. Despite certain blemishes, his record as a soldier was enviable. He was certain that one great victory over the Sioux, perhaps even the death or capture of Sitting Bull or Crazy Horse, would vault him into office.

"Yes," smiled Custer. "The Seventh Calvary will march on the Sioux, and with your support, victory will be mine." *And its glory and rewards*, he thought to himself.

"General, there are too many Sioux and Cheyenne in the valley of the Greasy Grass. Too many for the Seventh Cavalry alone," countered one of the scouts.

"You always exaggerate the enemies' numbers," replied Custer. "The Seventh is the greatest force of Indian fighters in the West. We'll have no problems." Even if the hostiles were met in unexpected numbers, the general was sure he could once again count on "Custer's Luck" to land on his feet.

"Remember, I'm depending on you," said Custer as they left.

On June 24, Custer called for his two senior officers, Major Marcus Reno and Captain Frederick Benteen, to discuss strategy.

"Reno, you take three troops and attack the upper end of the camp. While you have the Sioux engaged, I'll attack the lower end of the village with five troops. Benteen, you'll also have three troops to provide support for Reno. Don't arrive too soon. We want to lull the Indians into a false sense of security," directed Custer as he looked to Benteen. "We'll reconnoiter and attack tomorrow."

It was an odd strategy. Usually, there would be more reconnaissance before an attack, but Custer was not inclined to delay. And if the officers were aware that the date of Custer's offensive was a day before that planned by General Terry, they held their tongues anyway.

Reno's battalion led the attack on the afternoon of June 25, advancing on the Hunkpapa camp. Reno must have sensed that something was not quite right because the Natives did not scatter under the troops' fire. Although the elderly and children wailed as they fled, the warriors held fast. Following the initial confusion, the Hunkpapa rallied. Under the direction of Gall and Sitting Bull, who had delayed to retrieve his war shield, bow and arrows and to ensure his mother was directed to safety, they mounted a counterattack. Reno's troops had all they could handle, but he took heart when Natives' cries drew his attention to the east side of the river. Custer and his troops were visible. Reno thought that when Custer began his assault on the Cheyenne at the northern end of the camp, the pressure would be removed from his own men. Victory seemed only a matter of time.

But victory did not come. Even as the warriors were holding their own, a cry gave them greater courage.

"Crazy Horse is coming! Crazy Horse is coming!"

Crazy Horse had indeed gathered his warriors and was riding hard from the northwest. They came like a "big wind roaring," their "eagle bones screaming" yelling, "Hoka hey!"

As the Hunkpapa were joined by increasingly large numbers of Sioux, Reno's confidence melted away.

Iron Hawk, a participant in the battle, described the events: "Crazy Horse and his warriors made a dash for the soldiers in the timber and ran into them. When the warriors assembling close to the bank saw this movement and heard the yells of Crazy Horse's men, they advanced furiously with great yelling, coming down on the flank. The soldiers broke and ran in retreat, the Indians using war clubs as the principal weapon, a few using bows and arrows, most of the execution being by knocking the troopers from their horses, the Indians moving right in among them."

Crazy Horse charged into the fray, his war club rising and falling, chasing frightened Wasichus across the river.

"Too late!" Red Feather called to his brother-in-law Crazy Horse. "You've missed the fight!"

"Sorry to miss this fight," laughed Crazy Horse. "But there's a good fight coming over the hill," he added, pointing to the hill northeast of the Little Bighorn River. Crazy Horse saw Custer and his men although he did not know it that it was Long Hair. "That's where the big fight is going to be! We'll not miss that one!" shouted Crazy Horse.

Crazy Horse left the fight against Reno, whose men had abandoned their horses and sought shelter behind the trees and brush. Pinned down, all Reno could do was wait for Benteen's reinforcements. Crazy Horse rode through the camp, blowing his eagle bone whistle, collecting warriors.

"Hoka hey!" called Crazy Horse, who then shouted the cry of the Brave Hearts. "It is a good day to die!"

When he finally rode out of the north end of the camp, Crazy Horse led 1000 warriors. They splashed across the Little Bighorn north of Calhoun Hill where Custer's men were located and then circled back. The warriors settled in a ravine, where they kept Custer's flank busy. Gall and his few hundred warriors, who had also left the Reno fight, kept Custer's battalion occupied from the front while Two Moons and his Cheyenne attacked from behind. For a time, the battle was reduced to an exchange of gunfire from well-protected positions, but such fighting was not good enough for the younger warriors who longed to demonstrate their courage. White Bull, an Oglala, ran the daring line between the opposing forces. He challenged Crazy Horse to do the same.

"Hoka hey, brother! This life will not last forever!" shouted White Bull.

Crazy Horse saw him run the daring line several times. It was not an activity for older warriors—including the 35-year-old Crazy Horse—who had nothing to prove, but he found it impossible to sit and watch. He gave a sharp blow on his eagle bone whistle and charged out of the ravine. Bullets whizzed past him and raised clouds of dust around him, but he was not hit. The warriors took Crazy Horse's action as a signal to attack, and they poured out of the ravine and charged the hill.

As White Bull told it, "The Sioux were raked with a heavy fire. Many of us were killed by this volley. This made me very mad. The soldiers left their horses and fled on foot. Some did not retreat but stood their ground. We overran their position although the soldiers kept up a heavy fire."

But as the soldiers' ammunition ran low, and the warriors pressed, the tide turned. They were forced to fight hand-to-hand and didn't have a chance against the more experienced Natives. Before sundown, Custer and his 220 troops were dead. Crazy Horse deserved much of the credit.

Amos Bad Heart Bull's drawing of Crazy Horse and Sitting Bull from "The Battle of the Little Bighorn" series

As one of the warriors noted, "He was the bravest man I ever saw. He rode close to the soldiers, yelling to his warriors. All the Wasichus were shooting at him, but he was never hit."

With Custer's force crushed, the Natives turned back on Reno's battalion, which had been strengthened by Benteen's arrival. Perhaps Crazy Horse joined them, although that is unknown. When it got too dark, the Natives halted their attack, but with sunrise they began again with renewed vigor. When the guns were finally silenced, Reno and Benteen had lost some 50 men. More might have died had Sitting Bull not called an end to the fighting. There had been enough bloodshed.

With the battle over, the Natives counted their dead—30 warriors. Many dead Wasichus also lay on the ground. The Natives had killed more than half of Custer's force, but they did not know that they had also killed Long Hair because no Wasichu had the telltale flowing reddish-yellow locks. Unknown to the Sioux, Custer had shorn them prior to leaving Fort Lincoln.

The Sioux began their victory celebrations on the fourth day after the fight. Crazy Horse was not there as usual. Sitting Bull was, but he could not enjoy them.

When he was asked about his reluctance to participate, he replied with a heavy heart, "The young braves have taken the spoils of victory. They have taken the Wasichus' guns, clothing and horses. From this time on, they will covet his goods. They will be at his mercy; they will starve at his hands. The soldiers will crush them."

The outcome of the battle had been foretold in Sitting Bull's vision. The truth of his observation would soon be evident in the response of the Wasichus, who were all too anxious to satisfy American demands for revenge and for an end to the problem of the Sioux.

CHAPTER SIX

Never a Wasichu

THE NATIVES TOOK TIME to mourn their dead and to celebrate their stunning victory in the valley of the Greasy Grass, and then the bands dispersed. It was the usual way of things. They had come together to fight, in greater numbers than they ever had, and they had struck a convincing blow against the Wasichus. They had killed many and had proven their bravery. But victory and bravery were not enough to sustain a people. Unlike the soldiers, who had food provided by supply trains, the Natives had to hunt for food, and the resources in the Powder River country were not sufficient to feed the large camp. Crazy Horse and the Oglala moved east to *Mato Sapa* (Bear Butte). Sitting Bull and the Hunkpapa traveled north to the Yellowstone River. The Cheyenne traveled south of the Platte River.

Wherever the Natives went, their empty stomachs rumbled. The once-abundant herds of buffalo that had thundered across the prairies just years before had all but vanished. The government promoted the destruction of the herds because officials anticipated that hungry Natives would be submissive Natives, but it didn't need to offer much incentive. Eastern factories demanded buffalo hides for leather products. Fertilizer factories sought their skeletons. The

The killing of buffalo for sport, contributing to the decimation of
the herds and the collapse of Native cultures

industry was enjoying a boom with the staggering growth in agriculture. Railroads became a time-efficient and cost-effective ship-
ping solution. New high-powered rifles, like the .55 caliber Sharps,
could bring down the toughest bull at 1500 yards. As a result, the
1870s saw the slaughter of more than a million buffalo a year. Old-
timers lamented the disappearance of the buffalo, but for the Sioux,
who depended on it for their way of life, it was catastrophic.

While hunger pains were sharp, the Sioux soon had greater concerns. The defeat at the Little Bighorn steeled the army's determination to rein in the hostiles. As Black Elk put it, "wherever we went, the Wasichus came to kill us, and it was all our own country."

General Crook, biding his time at Goose Creek, finally put away his fishing pole in favor of a rifle, and he marched his men in search of Crazy Horse. In early September, a detachment under the command of Captain Anson Mills found American Horse's small band of 37 Sioux lodges at Slim Buttes on Rabbit Creek in northwestern South Dakota. The soldiers attacked at dawn, taking the sleeping camp by surprise. Few casualties occurred at the Battle of Slim Buttes but American Horse was fatally wounded. Most escaped, but they did so without the dried buffalo they had made for winter provisions.

Some of American Horse's band were captured, and under interrogation, they revealed that Crazy Horse's band of 700 warriors was nearby. Crook, who had arrived at Slim Buttes as the fight was nearing a close, knew that more Sioux were in the vicinity because Natives had been reflecting mirrors on the soldiers during the battle. He prepared his men for renewed fighting, which came late in the afternoon with the arrival of Crazy Horse, He Dog and many warriors.

The Sioux took positions on the hills overlooking American Horse's razed camp and opened fire. Eventually, Crook's men forced them from the hills. The opposing sides exchanged distant gunfire until nightfall. The next morning the Sioux renewed their attack, but Three Stars had had enough and ordered his troops to pack up. They headed south towards the Black Hills, taking several captives with them, including Crazy Horse's friend Little Big Man. Crazy Horse and his warriors nipped at their flanks during the retreat, but they broke off when Crook finally reached a supply column in mid-September. Crook claimed victory at the Battle of Slim Buttes, but it wasn't much of a victory. The Sioux know the battle as "The Fight Where We Lost the Black Hills." It was a name that emerged in hindsight.

Crazy Horse headed west with his band, eventually making camp on the Tongue River. But no relief was in sight. Black Elk remembered, "…the bison had gone away…and a hard winter came on early. It snowed much; game was hard to find, and it was a hungry time for us. Ponies died, and we ate them."

Heavy hearts joined empty stomachs. "We were not happy anymore," said Black Elk, "because so many of our people had untied their horses' tails and gone over to the Wasichus."

In the Moon of Falling Leaves (November), those heavy hearts were crushed when news arrived that *Paha Sapa* had been sold. Little about the sale was legal or ethical. The government appointed a commission and authorized it to make treaty to cede the Black Hills, the Powder River country and the Bighorn Mountains to the United States. When it was pointed out that alterations to the Laramie Treaty of 1868 required the signatures of three-quarters of the adult male Sioux population, the government declared that the number did not include the hostile Sioux. And to insure the consent of the agency Natives, the United States Congress withheld rations from them and prohibited off-reservation hunting. Throughout September, agency chiefs and headmen, including Red Cloud, Spotted Tail and Young Man Afraid of His Horses, touched the pen. *Paha Sapa* was gone.

But the Wasichus desired more than just land. The army wanted to crush the Sioux and their allies. In early fall of 1876, General Nelson A. Miles, known as Bear Coat to the Sioux because he wore a bearskin coat, built Fort Keogh on the Yellowstone River near the mouth of the Tongue River. Miles used the fort as his base of operations against the hostile Natives. In October, his troops caught up with Sitting Bull and the Hunkpapa near Cedar Creek, midway between the Yellowstone and the Missouri rivers. The two leaders agreed to parley, and when Sitting Bull refused Miles' demand that he surrender unconditionally, Bear Coat prepared his men to fight. The resulting Battle of Cedar Creek was yet another inconclusive fight. Sitting Bull and his followers managed to escape

General Nelson Miles (1839–1925) in 1876. He tried to prevent the Sioux escape into Canada after the Battle of the Little Bighorn.

by retreating to the Yellowstone River. But some of his followers were tired of fighting, and dreading the thought of a winter on the run, they surrendered.

General Crook, meanwhile, continued on Crazy Horse's trail. Under his command were 2600 men, with 300 Native scouts. Determined to defeat Crazy Horse and to avoid continued embarrassment, Three Stars sought to improve his odds by using Sioux scouts. Before heading out to the field, he traveled to Red Cloud Agency with a demand. The chiefs and headmen gathered in council to hear it.

"All warriors will have to sign on as scouts to fight Crazy Horse," declared Crook.

Spotted Tail, who had just been appointed agency chief by Crook, objected, "Sioux cannot fight Sioux. It is not the way of things."

"The government is feeding your lazy braves," boomed Three Stars, "and they should damn well get off their asses and start working for a living."

Crook's reddening face and angry words failed to convince the Sioux leaders.

"Fine," said Crook. "Then I will give each warrior who scouts for me a horse and a rifle."

Before he left the agency, Crook signed up 60 scouts. Among the first to accept the offer was No Water, Crazy Horse's old enemy.

The troops set out from Fort Fetterman in November, traveling north on the Bozeman Trail. They encountered Dull Knife's Cheyenne band along the Red Fork of the Powder River in the southern range of the Bighorn Mountains. Dull Knife had fought in the Battle of the Little Bighorn, but Three Stars' mood was such that the Cheyenne participation in that fight was unnecessary justification for engagement. The soldiers attacked at dawn on November 25, catching the Cheyenne by surprise. The soldiers killed 40 Natives, including women and children, many of them taken down by bullets before they could escape from their lodges.

The Cheyenne survivors of the Battle of Hole-in-the-Wall had neither supplies nor clothing and only a few ponies. They made their way northeast slowly, hoping to find Crazy Horse's camp along the Tongue River. But the short journey was difficult. The night after the battle, temperatures dropped to −30° F. Eleven babies froze to death, their mothers' desperate embraces providing insufficient warmth. Days later they stumbled into Crazy Horse's camp. What might have gone through the Oglala chief's mind can only be imagined. His band, still 2000 strong (with some 500 warriors) had hardly enough to feed themselves. Many children were sick and the elderly were weak. But the Oglala could not turn away the Cheyenne. The bands shared the Sioux's few supplies and ate from the same pot of boiled pony that was more marrow than meat.

Late in 1876, Crazy Horse began to sense the inevitability of the situation. He knew that he and his warriors might live on the run for many more months, fighting when possible, retreating when necessary. But he also realized that others in his band could not. They were tired, hungry and sick. Crazy Horse reflected deeply and at length on the best course of action.

They were bad times, remembered Black Elk: "After that, the people noticed that Crazy Horse was queerer than ever. He hardly ever stayed in the camp. People would find him out alone in the cold, and they would ask him to come home with them. He would not come, but sometimes he would tell the people what to do. People wondered if he ate anything at all. Once my father found him out alone like that, and he said to my father: 'Uncle, you have noticed me the way I act. But do not worry; there are caves and holes for me to live in, and out here the spirits may help me. I am making plans for the good of my people.'

"He was always a queer man, but that winter he was queerer than ever. Maybe he had seen he would soon be dead and was thinking how to help us when he would not be with us any more."

If Crazy Horse was contemplating his imminent death, he also realized that there remained responsibilities while he was alive. Throughout early December, the headmen of his band met often in council to discuss what should be done. Debate was less enthusiastic than it had once been.

"We should accept the offer brought by Important Man and Foolish Bear," sighed one of the Sioux. The two runners had been sent out from one of the southern Indian agencies. The message they brought promised that the hostiles would be welcome at the agency if they agreed to certain conditions.

"But they want our ponies and guns," replied He Dog. "How can we give them up?"

"What good are they to us? There is nothing left to hunt. Where can we ride on the reservation?"

"They say the Wasichus have promised not to punish us," added another.

"What punishment is greater than riding into the agency?" asked Crazy Horse. "The band will live, but not as Sioux."

All fell silent for a moment at the words of their chief.

"Better to live," suggested one.

"Then make plans to live," said Crazy Horse, who, despite his misgivings, knew that he was responsible for the well-being of the band. His personal desires no longer mattered. His people needed food, shelter and rest, and those could no longer be found in the Powder River country, especially while being chased by Wasichus.

On December 16, 1876, a small delegation of 25 Sioux and Cheyenne left the village and rode for Fort Keogh to meet with Colonel Miles, who considered Crazy Horse "the personification of savage ferocity." Crazy Horse was not with them. Perhaps he sensed Bear Coat's attitude towards him, but more likely Crazy Horse simply didn't trust the Wasichus. The delegation stopped some distance from the fort. Five men holding two white truce flags went ahead to parley with Bear Coat.

To get to Bear Coat, the party had to pass through a camp of Crow scouts. The Crow made friendly with the emissaries, smiling and shaking hands. But when they were fully inside the camp, the Crow attacked. During a brief hand-to-hand fight with much gunfire, the outnumbered Sioux were quickly killed. The Crow attack may have been because of a recent attack Crazy Horse had made on them, but the Crow needed little reason to fight their traditional enemies.

When Miles heard the gunfire, he ordered his men into the Crow camp. They arrived after the Sioux had been killed, and too late even to detain those responsible. They had quickly departed for their agency along the Bighorn River. Miles was incensed. Crazy Horse had slipped from his grasp.

"Goddammit!" he bellowed at the Crow. "You were told not to attack any Sioux messengers." He continued on, cursing a blue streak that the translator felt no need to interpret.

"Sergeant," he finally barked. "Disarm the remaining Crow and take 12 horses. And get someone here with a paper and pen!"

Even as he was berating the Native scouts, Miles was thinking of some way to recover from the disaster. He dictated a letter assuring the Sioux that the army had no part in the attack. The letter and the 12 confiscated horses were sent north to Crazy Horse's camp.

But the words of a Wasichu no longer mattered to Crazy Horse. It took little for him to convince those among his people who wanted peace that the Wasichus could not be trusted. The Sioux and the Cheyenne again prepared for battle.

〰〰〰

Days after the unexpected attack by the Crow on the Sioux delegation, Important Man and Foolish Bear returned to Crazy Horse's camp on the Tongue River. They remained hopeful that the Oglala chief could be convinced to lay down his war club and surrender at one of the southern agencies. Their hope was ill founded. The council met to discuss the matter, but the voices in favor of peace were fewer in number and less persuasive in their argument. Crazy Horse and his allies spoke of renewed resistance to the Wasichus. They had only to point to the recent treachery at Bear Coat's camp to confirm their suspicion that the Wasichus could not be trusted.

The council agreed to go on the warpath. They sent a bold message to Bear Coat, declaring that the band did not start this fight, but that it was prepared to fight for as long as it could. They made raiding plans and told Important Man and Foolish Bear to return to their agency. Crazy Horse ordered that none from the camp could go with them because he did not want Bear Coat to know of his plans. When some tried to follow the emissaries anyway, the *akicita* stopped them, killed their horses and confiscated their rifles. Crazy Horse realized that the freedom he gave his people in times of peace was a luxury that could not be granted during war. Then the band moved down the Tongue River because, as Black Elk said, "There was no better place to go." They waited for the Wasichus.

The Sioux first struck on December 26, raiding the army's herd of cattle. They stole 250 animals and ate well for the first time in months. The action angered Miles, who ordered his troops into action. During the last days of 1876, 450 soldiers marched up the Tongue River. At the same time, a war party led by Crazy Horse and Dull Knife made its way down the river. While a few minor skirmishes occurred in the first week of 1877, it wasn't until January 7 that the army finally closed in on Crazy Horse's camp near the Wolf Mountains. The most significant encounter of the campaign occurred with their arrival.

Scouts informed the Sioux and Cheyenne that the Wasichus were approaching their camp. Anxious to protect band members and their few supplies, the Natives decided to attack. Crazy Horse was hopeful on the morning of January 8. He had some 700 warriors, outnumbering the troops. And, as usual, the warriors were confident.

They taunted army scouts as the enemy went through their morning routine.

"You have eaten your last breakfast!"

"Wolves will be eating your flesh this night!"

"Cowards!"

It might have been better for the Sioux had they remembered the old Sioux adage to avoid a fight in the snow, which was a foot high on the ground that morning.

Miles expected the Sioux to attack, and he was ready for it. He had howitzers disguised as supply wagons, and he felt certain that the weapons would give him the upper hand. He was right. When the warriors swept down from the bluffs towards the army's camp, they were forced to hold under the superior firepower. As the soldiers pressed their advantage, some warriors retreated to the hills. For a time hand-to-hand combat ensued, which suited the Natives because they had limited ammunition for their weapons. The battle, however, was short-lived. A blizzard swept in, and engulfed the Wolf Mountains. Under cover of the blinding snow, the warriors returned to their camp, collected the women, children, elderly and the ponies, and hurried back up the Tongue River. The weather became so severe that Miles was forced to let them go after only a brief pursuit.

The Battle of Wolf Mountains (sometimes called the Battle Butte Fight) saw few lives lost—two soldiers and three warriors. But it was demoralizing for the Natives. They were forced to leave behind many of their meager supplies.

Black Elk remembered, "We got away, but we lost many things we needed, and when we camped on the Little Powder, we were almost as poor as Dull Knife's people were the day they came to us. It was so cold that the sun made himself fires, and we were eating our starving ponies."

The Moon of Frost in the Teepee (January) was a difficult one, but excitement rippled through the camp at the mouth of Prairie Dog Creek along the Tongue River a few weeks after the fight. Crazy Horse's greatest ally, Sitting Bull, arrived. He brought word of a new plan that might yet allow the Sioux and Cheyenne to avoid defeat.

Sitting Bull proposed his idea at council. "I see your camp. People are cold and hungry, much like my own band of Hunkpapa," he observed. "We have traveled throughout the Powder River country and the Elk River country; our bellies remain empty. The Wasichus are not hungry. They don't need to hunt and so they are always able to look for us. We cannot stay in one place long enough to get warm, to regain our strength. Even the warriors tire. How much longer can they fight these Wasichus?"

The Battle of Wolf Mountain, January 8, 1877, between General Nelson Miles and Crazy Horse's Sioux and Cheyenne

"Our warriors are brave!" countered one of the listeners. "They will fight."

"They will run because they have to run," replied Sitting Bull. "As sure as fire burns, to remain in one place is to invite death. Brothers, I do not doubt the bravery of the Sioux or Cheyenne," he continued, "but it is no longer a question of bravery. It is a question of survival."

"And how might we survive?" asked Crazy Horse. "Where might a man and his family live as Sioux?"

"Above the Medicine Line [in Canada]," answered Sitting Bull. "I believe that the heart of the Grandmother [Queen Victoria] is not hardened against us. It is said that the Red Coats [North-West Mounted Police] who rule on the plains do not raise their rifles against our people."

Sitting Bull listened to the murmurs of skepticism.

"It sounds unlikely, I agree. But we have no choice. We must hope. There is no longer hope to be found here."

"The Santee Sioux were given a reservation when they fled north years ago," added one of the Sioux headmen.

"Perhaps we might expect the same," suggested Sitting Bull. "We will be safe there. Let us cross the Medicine Line together."

The council fell silent. Most had assumed that Sitting Bull would propose that the bands join together and continue to fight. But to go to Canada? Perhaps it was a solution.

Crazy Horse broke the silence.

"My people are cold here. The wind blows even more harshly above the Medicine Line. Many would die."

"Many will die along the Tongue, brother, be it from the wind or at the hand of the Wasichus," replied Sitting Bull. "Above the Medicine Line we might grow strong again. The fight need not end."

"The fight *has* ended, brother," said Crazy Horse. "And it was not lost because the warriors fought without courage. Wherever we stop, the Wasichus find us and kill us. Well, we kill too. We have to protect ourselves. But warriors cannot fight on empty stomachs. They cannot fight when they know that to lay down their weapons means that their women and children might eat and be warm.

"What does it matter where we have a reservation?" continued Crazy Horse. "Wherever it is, we will be dependent on the Wasichus. They will tell us how to live, if life on the reservation can be called living. It will not be a life that I am familiar with. I do not understand the Wasichus. They are never satisfied. They always want more. But we will have to try and understand. It will be difficult, but I will try.

Hunkpapa Sioux chief Sitting Bull (1831-90) in 1888. Sitting Bull was a respected and feared warrior and a *wichasha wakan* who was granted a vision that foretold Custer's defeat at the Little Bighorn. In a desperate effort to remain free after that battle, Sitting Bull led his people to Canada in the spring of 1877. The North-West Mounted Police, the law in western Canada, considered the Sioux refugees well behaved, but the Canadian government wanted to avoid the expense of feeding them and ordered their return to the United States in the summer of 1881. When Sitting Bull was killed by agency police acting under the local Indian agent's directions, James Walsh, a retired Mountie and good friend of Sitting Bull, declared, "He asked for nothing but justice."

"Those who fight with me know that as a warrior I would rather die than go to a reservation. But as a chief, it is no longer my desire that matters. I cannot choose death for my people," declared Crazy Horse.

Then, after a moment of silence, he added hopefully, "Bear Coat will not attack while there is snow on the ground. We will be safe until spring. Perhaps Wakan Tanka will show us the buffalo by then."

"You are a fool," spat Sitting Bull, who rose and left the council. The Hunkpapa chief returned to his people and prepared for the journey across the Medicine Line.

Crazy Horse's band began to break up with the decision to remain in the Powder River country. It was impossible to find enough game to feed 2000 Natives. The Oglala and some Cheyenne followed Crazy Horse west to the Little Bighorn River, desperate to find animals to hunt. Others abandoned hope of finding game and, faced with a cold and hungry winter, they rode south and surrendered. When news of the condition of Crazy Horse's band reached agency authorities, Generals Crook and Miles saw an opportunity to bring in the hostiles. Both sent out runners to convince Crazy Horse to surrender. The largest was a delegation of 30 Oglala led by Crazy Horse's old friend Sword. His efforts proved ineffective.

The winter was cold, and many were suffering. Crazy Horse's band could no longer hold out. In early February 1877, runners from Crazy Horse's band arrived unexpectedly at Camp Robinson. The runners reported that if Spotted Tail, Crazy Horse's uncle and chief of the agency Oglala, was sent north to discuss terms, the Natives might be convinced to come into the agency. Crook had asked Spotted Tail to go north in January, but when Spotted Tail learned that he was to demand Crazy Horse's unconditional surrender, he declined the mission. In a month, the situation had changed. Spotted Tail knew that Crazy Horse would welcome him, so he agreed to go.

On February 13, Spotted Tail, more than 200 Oglala warriors and a few Wasichus, set out from Camp Sheridan near the Spotted Tail

Agency. They took many packhorses loaded with gifts. Crook refused to cut corners in his effort to persuade Crazy Horse to come into the agency. Weeks later the delegation found Crazy Horse's camp on Otter Creek, along the Tongue River. The messengers were informed that the band was traveling north to meet with Bear Coat to discuss terms of surrender. Spotted Tail, who knew that a successful mission would enhance his prestige with Three Stars, immediately began giving out ammunition. He promised that if the band surrendered at a southern agency, they would be permitted to keep some of their guns and horses to hunt buffalo.

But Spotted Tail did not make the offer to Crazy Horse, who was away hunting. Crazy Horse did not want to participate in council and his absence was true to form, but perhaps he also wished to avoid discussions that would result in his surrender. However, he knew of his uncle's presence and sent Worm, his father, to inform the council that he would agree to their decision.

Spotted Tail's offer was not accepted immediately. Despite their weakened position, the Sioux still tried to shape the terms of their surrender. Runners were dispatched to Bear Coat's camp to determine if he would improve upon the offer made by Three Stars. He wouldn't. The band couldn't decide on a united course of action, and it split up, with smaller groups making their own choices. The Oglala were virtually unanimous in their decision to follow Spotted Tail south. They agreed to go in the spring.

In early April, Spotted Tail returned to tell Crook the good news. Not everyone shared his pleasure. Lieutenant William H. Clark, the military authority at the Red Cloud Agency (near Camp Robinson), was jealous of General Crook. Clark wanted Red Cloud reinstated as chief of all the reservation Oglala (Crook had appointed Spotted Tail to the position) because he believed it would enhance the importance of his own agency. He suggested to Red Cloud that he be the one to meet with Crazy Horse and lead him to the agency. Red Cloud, who was jealous of Spotted Tail and supportive of any action that might improve his own standing, agreed enthusiastically.

Brulé Sioux chief Spotted Tail (1823–81), the brother of Crazy
Horse's stepmother. Initially, Spotted Tail opposed the white
man's intrusion into Sioux territory. His position changed after he
surrendered to General Harney because of an attack on a mail
train in 1855. Spotted Tail was imprisoned at Fort Leavenworth,
Kansas, and he saw so many white men on the journey there that
he concluded opposition was futile. Spotted Tail became an
advocate of peace, signed the 1868 Fort Laramie Treaty and was
made chief of his own agency near Camp Sheridan. When Crazy
Horse surrendered, Spotted Tail feared that Crazy Horse's
popularity might undermine his influence among reservation
Sioux, and he did little to help his nephew in the difficult summer
months of 1877.

NEVER A WASICHU   209

With 100 warriors, many presents and much food, Red Cloud made his way north in mid-April. He met up with the remnants of Crazy Horse's band on April 27. With no food and little energy, they traveled slowly. Red Cloud declared that he had news and wished to report it to a council.

"Red Cloud has been sent by the Great Father," declared one of the Sioux who accompanied him. "He will lead you to a reservation that has been set aside for you, where you can live in peace."

Crazy Horse's friend He Dog spoke for the Oglala: "We and other Indians were raised on this land. The Great Spirit of Wakan Tanka gave us this land. He created animals that we catch and make clothing for our people, and also the sweets that grow on trees. Wakan Tanka gave us this land to live on and protect as our own. You know what the Great Father and his soldiers do to us? They make war, burn our homes, our tents, wherever we may be, and kill our people. It is only right that we protect ourselves, our people, our country. The only thing we can do is protect ourselves and fight with the soldiers. We do not fight because we want to, but because we have to, to stay alive. We do not want to spill blood, either ours or the Wasichus'. Therefore, we agree with you. We will go back with you to live in peace with the white men and learn their ways."

With the speeches complete, Crazy Horse spread his blanket for Red Cloud to sit on. Then he gave Red Cloud his shirt. Everyone understood the meaning of the gesture. Crazy Horse had surrendered.

"It is enough," declared Crazy Horse to Red Cloud. "Let us go to Camp Robinson."

But even as they journeyed south, Crazy Horse reconsidered his decision. Some of the warriors were going to hunt buffalo.

"Lame Deer and others are going to shoot tipis," Crazy Horse said to He Dog. "I am going with them."

"You think like a child," chided He Dog. "You smoked the pipe of peace the same as I. You promised to go back with Chief Red Cloud and to live in peace with the Wasichus. Don't run away from our grandfathers. Do not do it. It is not good."

Crazy Horse said nothing, and the next morning he left with Lame Deer and the others. A few days later, however, he returned.

Red Cloud, meanwhile, had sent word to Lieutenant Clark at Camp Robinson that more food was needed to feed the 900 Oglala. Clark dispatched Lieutenant William Rosecrans and 50 Indian scouts with 10 wagonloads of rations and 100 head of cattle. In early May, the supplies arrived. Crazy Horse shook hands with Rosecrans, the first Wasichu to have that honor.

On May 6, Lieutenant Clark met Crazy Horse about two miles north of Camp Robinson. Crazy Horse gathered his headmen and they sat in a row in front of Clark. The Oglala chief then motioned to Clark to step forward. He took Clark's hand in his own left hand.

"Friend, I shake with this hand because my heart is on this side," he explained. "The right hand does all manner of wickedness; I want this peace to last forever."

"No matter how fierce or brave a person thinks he is, if he learns to humble himself once in awhile, he will be well liked and good things will happen to him," replied Clark.

Crazy Horse frowned at the Wasichu and then motioned to He Dog, who stepped forward and presented Clark with his own war bonnet. It was the traditional act of surrender, one that Crazy Horse could not make because he had never worn a war bonnet.

The formalities complete, the Oglala marched to Camp Robinson. To those who watched, they appeared as anything but a defeated people. Crazy Horse and He Dog led, and warriors followed, all painted and dressed for war. As they entered the White River valley, Camp Robinson came into view. It was quickly obscured by the thousands of agency Natives who poured out to greet them, lining the trail for nearly two miles. The Oglala passed between the lines, and the chiefs and warriors began to sing. The women and children joined them. Before the band reached the camp, the onlookers were also singing. They sang words of praise and respect for Crazy Horse.

An army onlooker declared, "By God, this is a triumphal march, not a surrender."

A drawing from *Frank Leslie's Illustrated Newspaper,* June 1877, of Crazy Horse and his band going to surrender to General Crook.

But all were not so happy, Black Elk remembered: "We had enough to eat now and we boys [he was 14] could play without being afraid of anything. Soldiers watched us, and sometimes my father and mother talked about our people who had gone to the

Grandmother's land with Sitting Bull and Gall, and they wanted to
be there. We were camped near Red Cloud's Agency, which was close
to the Soldiers' Town (Camp Robinson). What happened that summer is not a story."

Life at the agency was difficult for Crazy Horse, but the problem
wasn't so much that he was under the control of the Wasichus. He
had accepted that, although he never bent to their will. As Black Elk
said, "He would not make himself over to a Wasichu...."

Crazy Horse's difficulties stemmed from his reputation and how
others responded to it. Unexpectedly, he found himself the center of
attention. Only in his late 30s, he was already a legend, so young
warriors and soldiers alike sought him out. Some were surprised to
discover that he was neither humiliated nor crushed by the turn of
events.

Lieutenant Bourke, a soldier who visited Crazy Horse soon after
his surrender, noted, "The expression of his countenance was one
of quiet dignity, but morose, dogged, tenacious and melancholy.
He behaved with stolidity, like a man who realized he had to give in
to Fate, but would do so as sullenly as possible."

Crazy Horse also found himself the subject of attention from
army officials. He wasn't long at the agency when Lieutenant Clark,
operating on orders from General Crook, pressured him to join the
Native delegation that was going to Washington. Crook believed that
Crazy Horse's presence in the delegation would increase his own prestige. To encourage Crazy Horse, Crook suggested that his agreement
would ensure he was made chief of all the Sioux. But officials did not
understand the man. He was not interested in political power.

Officials sweetened their offer. Lieutenant Clark introduced
Crazy Horse to Nellie Laravie, the half-French, half-Native daughter
of a trader, and encouraged him to marry her. He did so. Rumors
also circulated that a buffalo hunt might be permitted. On May 15,
Clark appointed Crazy Horse as a noncommissioned officer in the

Oglala Sioux Black Elk (1863-1950) in 1936. He has been described as a mystic, a medicine man, a holy man and a *wichasha wakan*. He was granted the first of the many visions he used to help his people at age 9, and by his teenage years his reputation among the Sioux was widespread. Black Elk's visions had a profound influence on the Sioux's understanding of the Ghost Dance, the spiritual ceremony that first became popular around 1890. Later he toured Europe with Buffalo Bill Cody's Wild West Show. Black Elk was Crazy Horse's cousin and thought him "brave and good and wise." While he was likely too young to have fought with Crazy Horse, Black Elk was witness to most of the major battles of the mid-1870s.

United States Indian Scouts. The appointment paid well and increased Crazy Horse's prestige on the reservation. But he remained adamant that he would not go to Washington.

"You have my horses and my guns," declared Crazy Horse. "I have only my tent and my will. You got me to come here and you can keep me here by force if you choose, but you cannot make me go anywhere that I refuse to go."

Crazy Horse's reluctance to participate in the delegation stemmed from his suspicion of the Wasichus. Since arriving at the Red Cloud Agency, he had been negotiating for a reservation in the Powder River country where he hoped that his people could pursue a more traditional lifestyle far from the forts and Wasichus. Instead, the army insisted that he go north to the Missouri River. Crazy Horse feared that the Washington trip was a ploy to remove him from the agency so that his people could be moved to a reservation in his absence. Aware of his concern, Crook himself encouraged Crazy Horse to go to Washington. He suggested that Crazy Horse might have a better chance of getting his desired reservation if he presented his case directly to President Rutherford B. Hayes. He also promised that no one would be relocated until all the Sioux had come into the agency, which would not be until Crazy Horse returned. In June, Crazy Horse agreed to join the delegation on the condition that he was first given a reservation in Wyoming. Crook wouldn't agree to such terms.

Meanwhile, the Sioux planned a Sun Dance to honor Crazy Horse. He attended the celebration on Beaver Creek, near the Spotted Tail Agency, but he did not participate. Instead he watched as five dancers sacrificed their flesh for him and the future of the Sioux. Sun Dances usually ended with the departure of a raiding party, but the traditional practice was no longer possible. Instead, five large rocks were rolled down from Beaver Hill and arranged in a "V" shape. Crazy Horse listened as they were dedicated to him and the warriors who had danced.

Spotted Tail and Red Cloud were worried about the show of respect for Crazy Horse. They also had heard the rumors that Crazy Horse might be named head chief of the Sioux. They knew it would be a popular choice among agency Natives and realized that if Crazy Horse was made chief, their own influence with the Wasichus would erode. So they began to spread rumors about Crazy Horse, that he planned to escape and return to the Powder River country, where he would fight the Wasichus. Army officials posted soldiers in Crazy Horse's camp and ordered them to watch his every move.

General Crook continued to curry Crazy Horse's favor. In late July, he called for a council at the Red Cloud Agency. Lieutenant Clark read a prepared message from Three Stars. Eighteen Sioux would go to Washington and make their case against a reservation along the Missouri River. He also promised that the Sioux could participate in a buffalo hunt, as long as they returned within 40 days and did not cause any trouble. When the council drew to a close, Young Man Afraid suggested that the customary concluding feast be held at Crazy Horse's camp, near the Red Cloud Agency.

Red Cloud was infuriated and sent word to special agent Benjamin Shapp, appointed by the Commissioner of Indian Affairs. "You are asking for trouble. A feast at Crazy Horse's camp will increase his prestige and undermine my own authority among the Sioux. I have proven myself a friend to the Wasichu. Crazy Horse is not to be trusted."

Shapp forwarded Red Cloud's concerns to his superior. "Crazy Horse has constantly evinced feelings of unfriendliness towards the others; he was sullen, morose and discontented at all times; he seemed to be chafing under restraint; and in their opinion was only waiting for a favorable opportunity to leave the agency and never return. The time has come now. Once away on a hunt, he and his band of at least 240 braves, armed and equipped, would go on the warpath and cause the government infinite trouble and disaster. The other Indians these men represented had no confidence in him. He was tricky and unfaithful to others and very selfish about the personal interests of his own tribe. Any ammunition furnished them would be used for the destruction of the whites against whom they seemed to entertain the utmost animosity."

Crook, if he was aware of the report, did not place much stock in it. He was still convinced that Crazy Horse could be used to his own ends. In early August, he sent Lieutenant Clark to Crazy Horse with a proposal. Frank Grouard, also nicknamed The Grabber, translated it.

"To the west, the Nez Perce, under the leadership of Chief Joseph, have rejected government demands that they relocate to a reservation, and they have taken flight. General Crook believes that Crazy Horse and his great Sioux warriors can defeat them."

Crook thought the proposal was the best way to limit risk to soldiers, but Crazy Horse was not told this.

"I have been authorized to offer you a horse, a uniform and a new repeating rifle should you accept the mission," added Clark.

"If I go," replied Crazy Horse, "my lodges must come with me. We will hunt as we track the Nez Perce."

"The army needs only your warriors," said Clark.

"When I came in from the north and met with the officers and others on Hat Creek, I presented the pipe of peace to Wakan Tanka," stated Crazy Horse. "I said I wanted peace, that I wanted no more war. I promised that I would not fight against any nation anymore. I want to be at peace now. I have been asked to go out and fight the Nez Perce but I do not want to do that. I remember my promise to Wakan Tanka not to fight anymore.

"But I will do it," he declared finally. "I will go north and fight until not a Wasichu is left."

Clark stiffened when he heard the words. Crazy Horse did want to return to the warpath! His own words revealed the truth.

But they were not Crazy Horse's words. Grouard had translated Crazy Horse words inaccurately. Louis Bordeaux, another interpreter who was present, took Grouard to task.

"Crazy Horse did not say that he would fight the Wasichu! He offered to go and camp beside the Wasichu and fight with them until the Nez Perce were killed."

"That is not what I heard," shrugged Grouard.

"Then you are deaf!" shouted Bordeaux. "You misinterpreted what he said."

Some of the English-speaking Sioux who were present agreed with Bordeaux, but Grouard would not admit that he had gotten Crazy Horse's words wrong. An explanation for his alleged misinterpretation was never forthcoming. But Grouard had feared Crazy Horse ever since Grouard left the Oglala to fight with Three Stars back in 1876. Perhaps he was swayed by promises or anticipated rewards from Red Cloud, Spotted Tail or even army officials. Whatever Grouard's motive, word of Crazy Horse's desire to return to the warpath spread like wildfire throughout the agencies. Seeing an advantage, the politically astute Red Cloud and Spotted Tail fanned the flames. Suddenly uncertain about Crazy Horse's intent, Crook stopped the sale of ammunition to be used for the buffalo hunt, and a day later postponed the hunt itself.

By mid-August, the rumors circulating about Crazy Horse's desire to return to the warpath and fight the Wasichus reached General Sheridan. He ordered Crook to look into the matter. Crook called for a council in early September. It was to be held at White Clay Creek between the Spotted Tail and Red Cloud agencies. All Sioux leaders were required to attend. Crazy Horse's band held their own council to discuss whether or not they would participate.

At Crazy Horse's council, He Dog declared, "All who love their wives and children, let them come across the creek with me. All who want their wives and children to be killed by the soldiers, let them stay where they are."

He Dog's argument persuaded most that the band should participate in Crook's council. It did not, however, convince Crazy Horse. He was probably not even at his band's council, and while his absence was not unusual, many in his band were growing frustrated with what they considered his stubbornness. In the minds of some, Crazy Horse had a responsibility to lead in council just as he had on the warpath. His refusal to do that was driving band members away from him to the other agencies.

Crazy Horse, however, had his reasons. After the council, he asked He Dog to meet him in his lodge. As they sat, he pulled out a knife and a cigar from under a pile of blankets.

"These are presents brought to me by two visiting Wasichus who came to see me this afternoon," said Crazy Horse. "They told me they were army officers, but they did not wear uniforms. I don't think they were army men.

"I did not like the way they shook hands with me and I did not like their talk or their gifts. I think the knife means that trouble is coming. They shook hands with me as if they did not mean me any good. I fear there will be trouble at that council," Crazy Horse confided to his friend.

"Does this mean that you will be my enemy if I move across the creek?" asked He Dog.

Crazy Horse laughed. "I am no Wasichu! They are the only people that make rules for other people that say, 'If you stay on one side of this line, it is peace, but if you go on the other side, I will kill you all.' I don't hold with deadlines. There is plenty of room. Camp where you please."

He Dog left the lodge and moved with those who chose to follow him. A few days later He Dog received a request from Lieutenant Clark that they meet. Clark, who was worried about the rumors surrounding Crazy Horse, but still intent on enhancing his own position, remained hopeful that Crazy Horse could be convinced to go to Washington. Crazy Horse had made it clear that he was not interested in going.

He had recently told Clark, "I am not hunting for any Great Father. My father is with me, and there is no Great Father between me and the Great Spirit."

But Clark thought that pressure from his friend He Dog and a gift of supplies and food might prove persuasive. Crazy Horse rejected the offer and refused even to meet with He Dog. Instead he sent a message.

"Tell my friend that I thank him and that I am grateful, but some people over there have said too much. I don't want to talk to them anymore. No good would come of it."

Crook, meanwhile, was en route to the council at White Clay Creek. He was not aware of Crazy Horse's refusal to participate, but he was no longer sure that he could trust the Oglala chief. Nevertheless, Crook was an honorable man, and he was determined to give Crazy Horse a final opportunity to explain himself.

As his party approached the council grounds, it was met by Woman's Dress, who had long held a grudge against Crazy Horse. The soldiers knew Woman's Dress because he had lived and worked as a scout at Fort Robinson.

"Where are you going?" he asked those at the front of the party.

"We are going to a council on White Clay Creek."

"Don't go there with Three Stars," warned Woman's Dress. "When you hold this council at White Clay, Crazy Horse will come in there with 60 warriors and catch Three Stars by the hand, like he is going to shake hands, and he is going to hold on to him. Those 60 warriors are going to kill Three Stars and whoever is with him."

There has never been any evidence that Crazy Horse planned to do this.

Woman's Dress had just finished talking when General Crook arrived. The interpreter told Crook what had been said.

"What do you know about Woman's Dress? Is he reliable? Does he tell the truth?" asked Crook, who knew nothing of the relationship between Crazy Horse and Woman's Dress.

"General, this is a big undertaking and I could not say. I am going to leave it up to Baptiste Pourier, a man who is with me, and he will tell you," said the interpreter.

Pourier was related to Woman's Dress by marriage.

"Woman's Dress is a truthful man, and whatever he says is the truth," assured Pourier.

Lieutenant Clark spoke up. He had grown impatient with Crazy Horse and had concluded that Crazy Horse wanted to escape and fight.

"General, we lost a man just like you when we lost General Custer. We miss him, and we couldn't replace him with any man alive. Don't go to the council without protection," he argued.

"But what excuse can I use for failing to attend a council I have called?"

"You leave that to me."

Crook agreed, finally convinced of Crazy Horse's desire to cause trouble, and Clark sent the interpreter ahead to inform the chiefs that Three Stars had been recalled urgently to Camp Robinson. When the Native leaders heard the message, they set out for Camp Robinson. In the group were Red Cloud, Young Man Afraid, American Horse (the nephew of the American Horse killed at Slim Buttes) and No Water. Crook met with them and immediately addressed Crazy Horse's malicious influence among the Natives.

"You are being led astray by Crazy Horse's folly. You must preserve order in your own ranks. Crazy Horse must be arrested," declared Crook.

The chiefs took some time to discuss this and finally gave Crook their answer.

"Crazy Horse is such a desperate man that it will be necessary to kill him."

"That would be murder, and I cannot sanction it," replied Crook. "There is enough force at or near the two agencies to round up Crazy Horse and his whole band. More troops will be sent if necessary. But I count on you, who have demonstrated your loyalty, to arrest him. It will prove to your people that you are not in sympathy with the non-progressive elements of your tribe."

Before the meeting broke up, Clark allegedly promised a reward of $300 and one of his best horses to the man who killed Crazy Horse. Crook was apparently unaware of the offer.

But some other army officers also opposed the murder of Crazy Horse. When Colonel Luther Bradley, commander of Camp Robinson, learned that a price had been placed on Crazy Horse's head, he sent for Clark. Bradley ordered him to arrest Crazy Horse and send him to Omaha and then Fort Jefferson, south of Key West, Florida.

An irate Clark called for an interpreter to relay Bradley's order to the chiefs.

"Those Indians can hold nothing. Bradley has got hold of that council we had with the Indians today, so you go down to the Indian village right away and stop those Indians from approaching Crazy Horse. When you go down, tell them not to disturb Crazy Horse, but tell them to report to Camp Robinson before sun-up in the morning," Clark ordered.

Some 400 agency Natives arrived at Camp Robinson on September 3, 1877, as requested. Eight companies of cavalry joined them. The Natives were issued ammunition and weapons and told to arrest Crazy Horse. But when they arrived at his camp, he was gone.

〜〜〜

Crazy Horse had tired of the rumors and intrigue at the Red Cloud Agency, and he wanted to distance himself from the bad people who lived there. He decided to move his band closer to the Spotted Tail Agency, which he believed to be more peaceful. The band set up camp about three miles from the agency. The lodges were hardly assembled before trouble began.

Angry that he had missed an opportunity to arrest Crazy Horse, Lieutenant Clark sent a messenger to Camp Sheridan, the army post close to the Spotted Tail Agency, with an offer of $200 to any Native who arrested Crazy Horse. Red Cloud dispatched some of his own supporters to arrest Crazy Horse, but when they found him, Crazy Horse declared that he was not trying to escape and that he would not return with them. Instead, he went to the camp of Touch the Clouds, a Miniconjou chief whom Crazy Horse had known for 20 years. Touch the Clouds was one of the few he counted on as an ally

Miniconjou Sioux chief Touch the Clouds in 1877. He was seven feet tall and an ally of Crazy Horse.

since his surrender. Crazy Horse knew that he had to go to Camp Sheridan to inform the commander, Captain Daniel Burke, of his relocation, but he was not inclined to go there alone. Touch the Clouds and 300 warriors escorted him.

Upon arriving at Camp Sheridan, Crazy Horse was greeted by Spotted Tail and a large group of warriors. There was little evidence that Spotted Tail felt any love for his nephew.

"We never have trouble here!" Spotted Tail shouted. "The sky is clear. The air is still and free from dust. You have come here, and you must listen to me and my people! I am chief here," he declared. "We keep the peace! We Brulés do this! They obey ME! Every Indian who comes here must obey me! You say you want to come to this agency to live peaceably. If you stay here, you must listen to me! That is all!"

Crazy Horse did not reply. Instead, he turned and walked to Captain Burke's office. Clark and Agent Shapp had relayed much of what the commander knew about Crazy Horse, and as a result, Burke was suspicious of the Oglala chief. He insisted that Crazy Horse return to Camp Robinson. At first, Crazy Horse objected because he wanted to avoid the trouble at the Red Cloud Agency, trouble that he had not started. He wanted to be left alone in peace. But when Burke assured him that the army had no reason to harm him, Crazy Horse agreed to return. He would depart the next morning and ask officials at Camp Robinson whether he might move his band.

But the next day, Crazy Horse changed his mind.

"I am afraid something will happen," he told Burke. "You go and fix up the matter for my people."

"Again I tell you that the army has no plans to harm you. You owe it to your people to return quietly and peacefully to the Red Cloud Agency," replied Burke.

"I will go if this Wasichu comes with me," he said, pointing to Lieutenant Lee, the second-in-command. "He must tell the Wasichus at Camp Robinson all that has happened here. And tell them that I am welcome at the Spotted Tail Agency if the Camp Robinson commander authorizes the move."

"Lee will accompany you. He will ensure that you have an opportunity to tell the commander how you have been misunderstood and misinterpreted, that you want peace and quiet and no trouble whatsoever."

Crazy Horse started out later on the morning of September 5 accompanied by Lee, the interpreter Bordeaux, Touch the Clouds, about a dozen of his friends and some other Natives selected by Burke. About 15 miles out, small parties of Spotted Tail's warriors began to arrive. About halfway to Camp Robinson, the party was surrounded. Crazy Horse tried to escape, but Spotted Tail's warriors soon caught up with him. They ordered him to ride behind Lee.

Lee sent a rider to Camp Robinson asking whether Crazy Horse should be taken to the post or to the Red Cloud Agency. A reply came from Bradley, directing Lee to escort Crazy Horse to Bradley's office. Lee knew that the office was next to the guardhouse, and he suspected that Crazy Horse was to be arrested.

When the party arrived at Camp Robinson, they were greeted by thousands of Sioux. Lee did his best to ignore them, heading for Bradley's office. He entered the office with Crazy Horse and asked to speak to Bradley.

"There is nothing to discuss. Crazy Horse will be arrested and transported. Even General Crook cannot change the order," replied Bradley.

"But he was promised an opportunity to make his case to move his band near the Spotted Tail Agency," objected Lee.

"Promises are irrelevant," interrupted Bradley. "Turn Crazy Horse over to the officer of the day. Tell him to go with the officer of the day, and not a hair on his head is to be harmed."

Crazy Horse was pleased to learn that he would be safe. When he was directed to the officer of the day, Captain James Kennington, Crazy Horse warmly shook his hand. Kennington, two soldiers and Little Big Man, Crazy Horse's old friend, who had since become a member of the agency police, escorted him outside and towards the guardhouse.

Amos Bad Heart Bull's drawing of the murder of Crazy Horse at Camp Robinson in September 1877.

When Crazy Horse realized that he was going to be confined, he resisted. He pulled out a hidden knife and tried to flee. Little Big Man grabbed him, an action he never explained.

"Let me go! Let me go!" shouted Crazy Horse as he sliced Little Big Man's wrist.

Little Big Man fell to the ground, but other Natives rushed in to restrain Crazy Horse. Many in the crowd were shouting, but the words of some carried more weight than others.

"Shoot in the middle! Shoot to kill!" cried Red Cloud.

"Kill the son of a bitch!" barked Kennington.

Private William Giles thrust his bayonet towards the restrained Crazy Horse. It found its mark, stabbing Crazy Horse in the back near the left kidney.

"He has killed me now!" moaned Crazy Hose as he fell.

Some of the onlookers tried to lift him from the ground.

"Let me go, my friends. You have got me hurt enough," he whispered.

He Dog had arrived after the incident occurred and saw that a Native was about to shoot Crazy Horse, he stepped towards him and angrily told the Native to go away. After the man left, He Dog knelt next to his friend and covered him.

"I will get someone to take you back to camp, brother."

As he stood, He Dog saw Lieutenant Clark. He strode over to the officer.

"You promised in a treaty that we both swore to that nothing like this would ever happen again," shouted He Dog. "That there would be no more bloodshed."

He Dog slapped Clark across the face and then left the post.

Camp Robinson's doctor Valentine McGillycuddy arrived soon after. He made his diagnosis quickly. Crazy Horse would not see the rising of the sun.

When the soldiers tried to move Crazy Horse, his followers stepped in. They did not want him taken to the guardhouse. In an effort to defuse the situation, McGillycuddy hurried to Bradley to ask what should be done.

When Bradley heard what had happened, he replied, "Please give my compliments to the officer of the day and inform him that he is to carry out his original orders and put Crazy Horse in the guardhouse."

McGillycuddy left to inform Kennington of Bradley's order. As he approached the guardhouse, he met American Horse.

"Crazy Horse is a chief and he cannot be put in the guardhouse," he declared. Many threatening warriors stood around American Horse and gave credence to his position.

A pony drag pulling Crazy Horse's body to its final resting place, illustration from a fall 1877 edition of *Frank Leslie's Illustrated News*.

McGillycuddy returned to Bradley, who changed his orders when the doctor assured him that there would be many more deaths if Crazy Horse was taken to the guardhouse. Instead, he was placed in the adjutant's office.

A few others joined the dying Oglala chief, including his father Worm and his friend Touch the Clouds. McGillycuddy administered morphine throughout the evening. Around 10 PM, Crazy Horse asked Touch the Clouds to send for Lieutenant Lee, who arrived quickly.

Crazy Horse took Lee's hand in his own and said, "My friend, I don't blame you for this. Had I listened to you, this trouble would not have happened to me."

The words may have been the last Crazy Horse spoke. He died around midnight.

Later, Worm and one of Crazy Horse's stepmothers took his body to the Spotted Tail Agency where it was placed on a scaffold near Camp Sheridan. Eventually they placed the body in a box, fastened it to a pony drag and rode northeast. To this day, no one knows where Crazy Horse rests.

Crazy Horse was dead. He was brave and good and wise. He never wanted anything but to save his people, and he fought the Wasichus only when they came to kill us in our own country. He was only 30 years old. They could not kill him in battle. They had to lie to him and kill him that way.

It does not matter where his body lies, for it is grass; but where his spirit is, it will be good to be.

—Black Elk

Notes on Sources

As much as possible, the dialogue in this book is accurate and the accounts described are fictionalized as little as possible.

Ambrose, Stephen. *Crazy Horse and Custer*. New York: Doubleday & Co., 1975.

Black Elk. *Black Elk Speaks* (as told through John G. Neihardt by Nicholas Black Elk). 1932. Reprint, Lincoln: University of Nebraska Press, 2000.

Guttmacher, Peter. *Crazy Horse: Sioux War Chief*. New York: Chelsea House, 1994.

Hinman, Eleanor. "Oglala Sources on the Life of Crazy Horse." *Nebraska History*. Vol. 75, No. 1 (Spring 1976); pp. 1–52.

Hollihan, Tony. *Sitting Bull in Canada*. Edmonton: Folklore Publishing, 2001.

Sajna, Mike. *Crazy Horse: The Life Behind the Legend*. New York: John Wiley & Sons, 2000.

Sandoz, Mari. *Crazy Horse: Strange Man of the Oglalas*. New York: Knopf, 1941.

Utley, Robert. *The Lance and the Shield: The Life and Times of Sitting Bull*. New York: Henry Holt, 1993.

About the Author

DR. TONY HOLLIHAN is an educator, author and historian who has held a lifelong fascination with the historical and sometimes mythic figures of North America. Born in St. John's, Newfoundland, Dr. Hollihan developed his interest in history at an early age and pursued it at Memorial University of Newfoundland and later at the University of Alberta. He has a Ph.D. in the History of Education and a Masters degree in Canadian and American history. He continues to share his interest in history through teaching and writing. He is the author of several books in Folklore Publishing's Legends series, including *Kootenai Brown*, *Gold Rushes*, *Sitting Bull in Canada*, *Great Chiefs*, Volumes I and II, and the forthcoming title *Mountain Men*. Dr. Hollihan lives in Edmonton (where he dreams of the ocean) with his wife Laureen and their three sons.

FOLK LORE PUBLISHING

Where history comes to life

If you enjoyed *Crazy Horse*, you'll love these other great historical narratives from Folklore Publishing...

Great Chiefs, Volume I
by Tony Hollihan

Chronicled here are the lives of famous Native chiefs and warriors who grappled with the increasing encroachment of European settlers in the West. The author dynamically brings to life these remarkable leaders and the means they adopted in a desperate bid to protect their people. Sitting Bull, Chief Joseph, Quanah Parker, Red Cloud, Louis Riel and Sequoyah are featured.

$10.95 US • $14.95 CDN • ISBN 1-894864-03-4
5.25" x 8.25" • 320 pages

Great Chiefs, Volume II
by Tony Hollihan

Tony Hollihan weaves more spellbinding tales of the courageous chiefs and warriors of North America's western tribes who battled valiantly against the growing tide of European settlement on their ancestral lands. Geronimo, Tecumseh, Crowfoot, Plenty Coups, Wovoka and Crazy Horse are featured.

$10.95 US • $14.95 CDN • ISBN 1-894864-07-7
5.25" x 8.25" • 320 pages

Sitting Bull in Canada
by Tony Hollihan

This book recounts the story of Sioux chief Sitting Bull's retreat into Canada after the Battle of the Little Bighorn. The story centers on the friendship that developed between the fierce warrior and the celebrated Mountie Major James Walsh.

$10.95 US • $14.95 CDN • ISBN 1-894864-02-6
5.25" x 8.25" • 288 pages

Louis Riel
by Dan Asfar and Tim Chodan

Champion of a people or traitorous revolutionary? Political visionary or religious lunatic? Louis Riel remains one of the most ambiguous figures in Canadian history, a man who stood and fell for the Métis nation. Read about this fascinating western icon in a well-paced biography.
$10.95 US • $14.95 CDN • ISBN 1-894864-05-0
5.25" x 8.25" • 232 pages

Gabriel Dumont
by Dan Asfar and Tim Chodan

This legendary buffalo hunter and warrior roamed the Canadian plains when buffalo were still plentiful and the Métis ruled the plains. The story of Louis Riel's mighty general is recounted here.
$10.95 US • $14.95 CDN • ISBN 1-894864-06-9
5.25" x 8.25" • 232 pages

Kootenai Brown
by Tony Hollihan

John George "Kootenai" Brown could boast countless adventures: serving in the British Army in India, hunting buffalo on the plains of Manitoba, riding Pony Express for the U.S. Army and fighting as a staunch conservationist in the region that eventually became Waterton Lakes National Park. Follow along in this exciting account of Kootenai Brown's incredible exploits.
$10.95 US • $14.95 CDN • ISBN 1-894864-00-X
5.25" x 8.25" • 256 pages

Look for books in the *Legends* series at your local bookseller and newsstand or contact the distributor, Lone Pine Publishing, directly. In the U.S. call 1-800-518-3541. In Canada, call 1-800-661-9017.